SLEEPING YOUR
WAY TO SUCCESS

SLEEPING YOUR WAY TO SUCCESS

How You Can Use Your Sleep Time to Speed You to Ultimate Life Success

JUDY MAY MURPHY

POOLBEG

Published 2008
by Poolbeg Press Ltd
123 Grange Hill, Baldoyle
Dublin 13, Ireland
E-mail: poolbeg@poolbeg.com

© Judy May Murphy 2008

The moral right of the author has been asserted.

Typesetting, layout, design © Poolbeg Press Ltd.

1 3 5 7 9 10 8 6 4 2

A catalogue record for this book is available from the British Library.

ISBN 978-1-84223-398-6

New Dream™, New Dreaming™, New Dreamed™, are all trademarks

Typeset by TYPE DESIGN in Sabon 11.5/16pt

Printed by
CPI Cox & Wyman, Reading RG1 8EX

www.poolbeg.com

ABOUT THE AUTHOR

Judy May Murphy is a world-renowned success coach and author of many internationally published books. She has a degree and masters from Trinity College Dublin and is an expert in many areas including NLP, Enneagram, Psychology, Hypnosis, Nutrition and Wealth Building. As a speaker and author she has coached and lectured to hundreds of thousands of people, helping them to achieve their best possible life, and has appeared on many television and radio shows. Judy May Murphy currently lives between Paris and Dublin.

ACKNOWLEDGEMENTS

With great thanks to all at Poolbeg for turning this project around in less time than they are usually afforded. Also to you, the reader, for taking action to make your life a masterpiece.

ACKNOWLEDGEMENTS

To Peter, Doris, Ben, Mark and Helena,
my Dream Team

CONTENTS

INTRODUCTION

*"When I woke up this morning my girlfriend asked me,
'Did you sleep good?' I said, 'No I made a few
mistakes.'"* — STEPHEN WRIGHT

For most of us, sleep can seem like a cruel and unusual arrangement. We have trouble getting into it; we remember only the odd highlight or lowlight; we have difficulty getting out of it even when the alarm goes off (or our toddler turns our eyelid inside out). After this, we promise ourselves vaguely that we'll somehow do better next time around.

Sleep is not as easy as it looks. And poor sleep is as big a problem as bad diet today.

Many people are so deprived of regular good-quality sleep that they have no idea how impoverished their lives are due to the decisions they have made, or have failed to make, around their sleep time. Like many people who have lived on junk food for so long, they have no idea how great it feels to be nourished and energised by fresh, live food. If constant lack of good sleep showed on our bodies in as profound and obvious

1

a way as lack of good food, perhaps we might be taking it more seriously. You will find thousands of books on how to eat well and only a handful on the joys of sleeping in ways that optimise your life. Think about it: one third of our lives are spent sleeping and we only ever talk about it to share a nightmare, or moan about how we didn't get enough sleep, or to apologise for sleeping late.

Bizarrely, people often wear their failure to sleep well as a badge of honour: "I'm so busy these days I'm only getting five hours' sleep a night," they will boast, putting themselves in the same category as Napoleon, Margaret Thatcher and other leaders around whom the myth of non-sleep was woven. If that same person were to announce that they were so busy that they were only eating doughnuts, or so busy that they completely ignored their family and friends, or so busy that they only drank half the amount of fluids needed, we'd be more likely to frown on their life strategy.

Take a second and think of your image of a successful person. It probably involves the notion of them being up with the lark and burning the midnight oil. In our society, sleeping has largely become associated with lazy under-achievers snoozing in front of the TV with a beer in one hand while a pizza falls off their knee to the floor. Sleep is seen as a waster of time, time that could be better spent making money, making love or making plans.

Is nobody calling a halt on this crazy minimal-rest

fest? The medical and coaching professions have always known that a lack of good quality sleep leads to disease, stress, poverty and depression while, conversely, adequate rejuvenating sleep leads to good health, good moods and the ability to function in ways more conducive to success. (Strange, then, how often being a doctor is synonymous with working 48 hours straight at a time!) Given that energy, co-ordination, clear thinking and good health are basic ingredients for getting great results in life, it seems basic to profess that being a successful person requires being a successful sleeper.

As a matter of course, in a structured or a random way, we learn many necessary and varied skills such as how to touch-type, how to drive a car or how to apply for a mortgage. Yet rarely, if ever, do we look at how we sleep and the impact it is having on our lives. If there were a test on sleeping, how would you do? Would you want to learn to do it better?

Similarly, we plan for holidays, we design the new kitchen, we have career goals, yet few people sit down and make firm goals for how they want to sleep. Instead, people often wait until their sleep is so disrupted that they cannot even function, before they take action to improve it.

There is so much that each of us wants to achieve, so many dreams and plans that are still more in our heads than in our lives. We want more money, more passion, a better family life, university degrees, published books, to have a literate and happy community, more time to play, adventure, castles, yachts and fancy cars. We each have a unique mission that only we can carry forward and these goals are not only wonderful, they are integral to the growth that we are here on earth to experience. Sleeping your way to success is about how to reach those goals using simple tools for reconditioning and rejuvenation that have been (until now) largely unknown, unrecognised and unused throughout modern times.

However, it takes more than effort and ingenuity to achieve these things you need and want. The necessary extra ingredient is TIME. It takes hours, days, weeks and years. And how frustrating that there are only twenty-four hours in the day and you have to sleep for seven or eight of them! Do you ever think that if only you could have those hours back again, you could effortlessly achieve everything you have set your heart on? Well, now you can.

In this book, you will learn how you can use that precious time that you are asleep to programme your brain for being more effective and successful during the waking hours. You will also become skilled in how to structure and plan your sleep so that you feel physically amazing – no matter what your sleep challenges have been in the past. Quickly and effortlessly, you will be able to design your sleep so that it maximises your success through playing with your dreams and having an amazing sleep routine. (And there is a lot more to that than just getting to bed early with a mug of cocoa!)

Sleep is of vital importance when it comes to taking stock of where you are currently in your life and the results you have been getting until now, in addition to making the fun and fast changes that will get you to where you could ultimately be. Whatever it is that you want more of – money, houses, love, health, good-looks, creativity, peace – and whatever it is you want less of – struggle, pain, illness, poverty, disappointment – it can all change here, tonight, while you are sleeping.

Most people have already tried numerous ways to become more successful in certain areas of their life, only to have been frustrated and discouraged. This is usually because they are battling against the natural flow of things, pushing instead of steering themselves toward where they would like to be, swimming upstream into madness instead of floating downstream to the desired destination. When we allow our natural selves to take over during sleep time, we can start to tap into our real power.

The first part of the book deals with the ways you can harness your dreams and the messages they send to speed you to success. The second part is about the strategies you can use to ensure you have the most powerful night's sleep possible and so are ready to manifest that success during your waking hours.

Wishing you sweet dreams and sweeter success.

PART ONE

IN YOUR DREAMS

ONE

TRUTH FROM DREAMING

"In dreams and love there are no impossibilities."
— Janos Arany

Okay, I'll come clean. A couple of years ago I used to think that an interest in dreams marked a person out as a granola-crunching tie-dyed goof, some big old suburban hippy. Dream catchers, dream journals, dream therapies, lucid dreaming, dream interpretations . . . lovely if you lived in India or New Mexico, but some of us had real lives to live!

My own focus was firmly on the setting and achieving of solid goals, building wealth, working out, attracting a soul mate – all of which seemed to reside at the opposite end of the spectrum to the dream world. My belief was that dreaming was for dreamers, while measurable action in the realm of reality was what would lead to my living a completely successful life. (I was more Madonna than Joni Mitchell.)

And here I am, writing a book on how to use dreaming to boost you to greater success. What happened?

Thankfully, I woke up to the power of sleeping and a realisation about how your dreams can be used to manifest those millions of euros, that top model body, seventh-heaven family, or whatever it is you truly desire.

So how did this turnaround of soap-opera unlikeliness come about?

I was doing pretty well by anyone's standards. I was finally going out again socially after some time-out to lick some imaginary wounds; I'd had two books published in Ireland, had just given up script-writing and occasional performing on television as my life-coaching business flourished; and was, for the most part, in good shape and great spirits.

Then one morning I awoke from a dream that irritated me beyond reason.

This dream consisted of me being miserable in the back seat of a taxi, being driven through a bustling, colourful marketplace full of people having more fun than baskets of fruit and veg would ordinarily induce. The dream taxi pulled up outside an empty hotel and, rather than paying and getting out, I simply moaned at the driver, "You see, I'm just so lonely." It was at that moment that I woke up, feeling as lonely and wretched as I had in the dream.

My usual form would have been to shake off a bad dream like a lapful of popcorn crumbs and get down to my oh-so-important tasks for the day. However, on this particular morning, I was too angry to let it go. It touched a raw nerve because, for so long, "I'm lonely" had almost been a mantra for me. As part of my self-development for the previous four years I'd been spending enormous amounts of time and energy focusing on and nurturing really close friendships. The "real" me had finally begun to feel wonderfully connected to people and to feel cherished and loved, and yet here was my dream spinning out this "lie".

As I lay there, awake but groggy, I decided to re-script the dream and run a brand new movie in my head, just to show my unconscious mind who was boss! In my New Dream I included some friends in the taxi with me, all of us laughing and singing enough to give the fun-lovin' market people a run for their mangoes. When the taxi pulled up outside the hotel, I imagined there were swarms of friends, family members and equally enthusiastic strangers waiting there for me. Before getting out, I smiled at the driver and explained, "I used to think I was lonely, but now I know I've always been surrounded by love." This version felt much better, so, still awake and lying there, I ran this version over a few times, until I eventually got out of bed feeling great. This was the first time I actively took an old dream and replaced it with a new one, taking command of what my unconscious mind was doing, redirecting it to a better place.

Casting off a discouraging emotion and replacing it with a far better feeling is a fantastic enough feat in itself, but in addition to this my research and personal experience had already shown me that good feelings magnetise your desires towards you. However, I also suspected that there was even more going on than the flicking of an emotional switch. When you feel great you are more attractive to others (in all ways) and are more relaxed and open to receive or take advantage of the opportunities that present themselves. You also have more energy to transform and grow your vehicles for attaining your desires.

Although my day-to-day life was now full of love and friendship, I had to acknowledge the importance of the fact that for so many years I had conditioned myself in the belief and identity that I was a lonely person, somehow apart from the crowd on every occasion.

A few years prior to that night, I'd had my first novel published, a story about two young women connected only to themselves and their mad fantasies. It defined loneliness. The force of that conditioning meant that the old pattern was still stored somewhere, was still an ingredient in my reality and it was that which made it possible for my dream self to say, "I'm just so lonely." Fine, so I might have done a great job emotionally and intellectually distancing myself from the old patterns, beliefs and mental processes, but that didn't mean it had ceased to be a part of my make-up.

So I found myself following the advice of the poet WH Auden, who said, "Learn from your dreams what you lack." And as a life coach I also added, ". . . and then make it better." It's like when you have lost weight but still reach for the slightly baggy clothes, or when you have an abundance of money for the first time in your life and still spend twenty minutes walking to another supermarket to be able to buy a bag of potatoes for a cheaper price. Sometimes the things that used to be part of our make-up can linger, making it harder for us to move forward into better places.

We all have things in our lives and about ourselves that we would love to make different and better. The root of this involves changing a core belief, value or emotional habit. Many people feel that success is a question of two steps forward and one step back. This "one step back" is the result of outmoded habits and behaviours that are linked to things we have stored in our unconscious mind, things that we do and feel on automatic pilot because of our early life conditioning.

Soon after that morning of dreaming my dream anew, I was talking with a friend who was very passionate about creating huge wealth in his life. He realised that a part of him wanted the wealth and yet another part of him was acting the way his father had always acted, being overly suspicious of any wealth-building opportunity, waiting and weighing his options for so long that each new avenue that his passionate side unearthed, his old cautious side then closed down. The "old stuff" was lurking, seeming to sabotage his efforts, whereas really it was a case of different parts of his mind being equally committed to opposing strategies. Once he realised this, he was able to start to intensify the new passion and delete the old programming, so it was two (and more) steps forward all the way. He was able to use New Dreaming as a part of his self-reprogramming.

OVER TO YOU

Take a couple of minutes to check in with yourself. After all, just hearing about other people's changes may be inspirational, but making your own changes will facilitate powerful new developments in your life.

What are the emotions and values in your life that you have identified need changing, and have been absolutely committed to changing, and yet it seems to be a constant case of two steps forward, one step back?

Fill in the blanks: *On one hand I* _____, *while on the other hand I* _____.

If loneliness, anger, poverty (lack), overwhelm, fear or any other debilitating emotion, is still even a small part of you, that means there still exists some internal struggle. You could be unintentionally threatening your success in that area, or at least not living the new way to its full potential. As I had been, you could be Jekyll and Hyding with your emotions.

Most of us want to change something material in our lives – to have more money, more free time, to be married, to live in a different country, to be more slender, to achieve a certain position in our careers – in the hope that we will then feel better emotionally. However, all the action we take often doesn't seem to make a blind bit of difference. The reason is that our emotional make-up is acting as an invisible barrier. The angry person is too tense to instil confidence in a business setting; the lonely person is giving off vibes of desperation to a potential mate; the anxious or demoralised person is more likely to be reaching for the biscuit tin than taking action to achieve a goal. So in order to instigate consistent and lasting change through intelligent action, we must first change the limiting emotion. Only when someone feels complete and content in themselves can they attract a healthy life partner; only when someone stops living in a state of panic about finances will they start to attract the people and circumstances that will allow the money to flow to them.

OVER TO YOU

Decide on what is the biggest belief about your emotional make-up that you've been trying to change or have wanted to change for some time. If you can't think of an emotion right now, decide on a behaviour you would like to change. It might be that you overeat, or argue with your spouse, or stay in a rut with your job. Keep in mind that most behaviours or "things we do" can be traced back to a feeling, so if you drink too much alcohol, this might be as a result of your feelings of worthlessness; while your reluctance to remove your butt from the sofa might stem from feelings of hopelessness.

- **STEP ONE:** Write down that negative emotion, feeling or behaviour.

- **STEP TWO:** Think about all the positive ways your life and the lives of those around you would be impacted if you were to replace that feeling or behaviour with a more positive one on a permanent basis. Perhaps you will be able to have that passionate relationship if you let go of mistrust and replace it with absolute faith. Or maybe if you rid yourself of constant feelings of lack and instead allow yourself to feel protected and lucky, you'll feel confident in taking a leap and leaving your job and will start to create great wealth in an area you love. So, you have written up the old and new feelings and how the change will help you and those you love.

- **STEP THREE:** Now write down all the ways you and your loved ones would suffer in the future if the problem were to continue. Really allow yourself to feel the pain of what you will experience if you don't take things in hand right now. After doing this (and I trust you have because I know that your loved ones and your dream are important to you), you will now be feeling the importance of adjusting what's going on in your mind, the importance of changing what you believe and how that makes you feel. So, how do you achieve this part? Read on . . .

After I "New Dreamed" the taxi dream I spent the morning thinking about what had happened, and with a bit of soul-searching realised that I did indeed still believe, in a small way, that I wasn't as close to my new friends as other people were to theirs, that I was still somehow on probation and as a result was overly pleasing them out of fear of being turned back to what still felt like my rightful place on the outskirts. Because of this, I would pull back when I felt I'd spent too much time with one person, just in case they would tire of me; I would also travel alone, assume relationships wouldn't last, and indulge in other "lonely girl" activities. There was a danger that my old "loner" identity could overpower my new "loved and cherished" identity if I didn't pay attention.

I wondered: could this "New Dreaming" I had just landed on be a way to rapidly rev up that process of creating an empowering, ongoing "new self"; a way to speed up the process of establishing and conditioning long-lasting change-for-the-better?

17

By New Dreaming, I had reinforced, in my own mind, the idea that I am someone who is surrounded by loving people and that we are, all of us, fully part of each other's lives. As a result of that fateful morning, I found myself within the next few hours picking up the phone and calling people I had lost contact with over the previous few months, and I e-mailed another friend to let her know that I would be coming to her birthday party after all. I felt differently and, as a result of this, I automatically took different action. Once I confirmed the fact that I am loved, loving and connected, I could effortlessly and without any force behave the way such a person tends to behave.

I became excited at the thought that there might be other old, limiting beliefs about myself that lay hidden under the surface. I recognised that once I transformed these beliefs, I would begin to fly even higher in all areas of my life.

I began to see how, with a little playing, New Dreaming has the power to transform us all into people who effortlessly achieve enormous success in all areas of our being.

By running the new version of the dream, I had fashioned a whopping great broom and brushed out the old cobwebs from where they stubbornly clung to the far corners of my deeper self. While New Dreaming, I was both clearing away the old pattern of loneliness and reinforcing the new pattern of sociability. I was letting myself know on a conscious and unconscious level that the old way is out and the new way is in. Obviously, having a complete idea of myself that says, "I'm fully loved and connected" serves me better than having two parts ("I'm not lonely" and "I'm lonely") tugging in opposite directions.

Similarly, having a full identity of healthy eater serves you better than being sixty per cent veggie-head and forty per cent burger-boy. Being a consistently confident person is better than getting out and living life to its fullest one day, and then crawling back behind a copy of some tabloid rag and a pastry the size of a small dog the next day, whining that you just can't cope.

In what areas of your life do you feel the tug? Some call this sabotage but really it is just that your "better" attributes need to become a greater part of you.

Are you buying stocks and shares one week and calling the home-shopping channel to buy more kitchen gadgets than there are recipes the next week?

Are you spending time with your kids on the weekend and ignoring them midweek?

Are you in a great mood in the morning and a grouch by dinnertime?

Are you planning your own successful business during lunchtime on Monday and then picking up your current boss's dry-cleaning after hours on Wednesday in the hope that your paltry Christmas bonus will be bigger this year?

Where is your tug? At work, at home, in terms of your health, your finances, your creativity, your spiritual growth?

How many times have we all decided on a new habit for ourselves, and, with all the best intentions, still slipped back into the old way? How many times have we stopped and then re-started smoking or drinking, eating sugary foods again, gone back to Saturdays of non-stop TV sports, decided to invest in buy-to-let property and then become distracted by trivial activities, or been a dedicated *Kama Sutra* lover for a week before reverting to missionary tactics? This is because our whole self, our complete identity, is not yet fully on-side. We need to condition and strengthen our new beliefs and behaviours until they become 100 per cent part of who we are.

The key is in the fact that all of us act in a way that is consistent with who we really believe ourselves to be, and what we believe about our world. No matter what the starting point, we become who we believe we are. For example, if you believe you are a loving person, then you are more likely to smile and speak kindly to people than if you believe yourself to be an anti-social grump. If you start off believing you are not a sociable person, even if you decide to be sociable from now on, it might feel awkward for the first while because you think this new behaviour is somehow fake and that people will see through it. If you were able to *fully* believe that you were this new lovely person, with no doubts getting in the way, then behaving and acting in that new way would be effortless, the smiles would be real and would happen spontaneously and the laughter would be unforced.

SOMETHING TO THINK ABOUT

Imagine you have been driving on the left-hand-side of the road for years when suddenly a relocation to France or Italy means you now need to drive on the right. In fact, not driving on the right will seriously damage your ability to live your best life or live life at all. At first, if you are not concentrating to some degree, there's a huge chance you will veer back over to the wrong side. Without road signs, constant vigilance and clues from other right-hand-side drivers, the tendency would still be towards the left until such a time as the right-side conditioning became stronger. It's not just a question of telling yourself once or twice, "Okay, I now drive on the right." It does take time to recondition yourself. So imagine being able to do that both on the road and in your bed, reinforcing through goal-setting, taking practical action, following what others do and also by New Dreaming.

Some people read self-help books or make a big effort to improve in some area by attending a coach, a trainer or a seminar, only to complain one blink-of-an-eye later that they find themselves back at square one. The secret lies in letting the deeper, greater "us" know that we have changed, not just letting the smaller conscious part of ourselves in on the fun. Imagine that your head consists of a hundred little people all running around following your orders. Imagine if only the ten of them working on the conscious floor got the message that you were now on a mission called "Rich and Sexy", while the other ninety who work on the unconscious floors were still running the old game-plan of "Broke and Sloppy". Your dreams would soon let you know that the "Broke and Sloppy" anthem was still being merrily sung, providing you with the opportunity of sending in a strong message to the "men" that the new orders are to do "Rich and Sexy" to the extent that paint will peel from the walls as you pass by and mere mortals will faint at your very presence. When you have most of the little people in your head moving in the same direction, success is nigh.

Take a minute and make a note of some more ideas on what your "right-hand driver" old beliefs and emotions might be and some "left-hand driver" new empowering beliefs and emotions that you might like to condition-in instead. Would you like to go from timid to courageous, from fearful to trusting, from lethargic to energised, from angry to peaceful, from bored to curious, from despondent to excited, from stressed to relaxed? What message does the majority of your head still need to get?

Take the notes you made from the earlier exercises in this chapter and see how much you can add to what you realise about your old ways and how you now choose to change these so that you are singing from one hymn-sheet, finally in harmony with your own head.

I was now getting excited knowing that New Dreaming could speed up my journey and make it more enjoyable and instructive along the way. Even with that first shot at it, I experienced a profound shift in the way I felt towards my relationships with others; I felt more connected to people even though I was physically on my own at the time. I realised that the dream had given me clues as to what I was still unconsciously feeling and I was then able to use those clues to recondition myself more strongly into the new way.

New Dreaming is when you take an old dream and recreate it so that it is in alignment with the way you would prefer things to be. You might take a dream about not having a car and walking in the rain and give yourself a Bentley in the New Dream or wings to fly above the clouds. You might find yourself waking up after a dream about falling and in the New Dreaming give yourself a strong rope or harness and let your unconscious mind know that slipping without a safehold is something that belongs in the past.

Since then, I have New Dreamed myself into better relationships, a healthier and fitter body, a more prestigious career, much more advantageous financial circumstances, greater adventures, and countless more empowering emotions, all of which have become a natural part of my life far more quickly than was happening before I began New Dreaming. Once I began sharing it with friends, family and clients, they also reported dramatic results. Of course, although it is hard to prove scientifically, I will be explaining it in terms of accepted psychology, mind technologies and dream-therapies all in easy-to-grasp ways, but the best thing is to simply give it a go yourself and notice the difference.

How do you New Dream?

As you wake and remember a dream from the night before, remain lying there and simply notice how you feel about the dream. Ask yourself what you would like to change about the dream to make it more in line with your ideal life. Then, using the basic model of the dream, rerun it (while still awake and lying there) making the changes you desire and allow yourself to really enjoy your new creation. It's like daydreaming a rewrite of the original. (Those of you who have trained as lucid dreamers might be able to complete this process by falling back asleep, but most of us will be half-awake or fully awake as we do this.)

If you were alone in your dream you might want to add a soul mate beside you; if you seemed to be in a smaller house than the one you desire, just push back those walls and redecorate; if your dream feels messy, tidy it up; if your dream is the wrong colour, change it . . .

whatever feels right to you. Whatever great things appear in your life have had the groundwork laid for them hours, days, months or even years before. New Dreaming steps up that process of laying the groundwork. It is putting out there a model of how you would like your life to be and preparing you to be the type of person you need to be in order to attract and live that life.

I began to New Dream most mornings on waking, thrilled that night-time was now as productive and vital to my success as daytime was.

One night I dreamed that a man who had been a popular classmate at university came up to me and asked how I was doing on the test, and I replied that I hadn't even started the test yet as I couldn't find my other shoe. The entire dream was of me scrabbling around for my missing shoe while he, and others in the class, got on with their seemingly simple task of passing exams. Rather than trying to work out where in my life I might be feeling like a non-starter, I lay there, only just awake, and re-imagined the entire scenario with me wearing two shoes and having fun easily writing answers to the questions. Armed with a feeling of triumph and unstoppability, I found myself looking forward to the work of the day ahead and hit the ground grinning. Over the next few weeks I could feel how the New Dreaming was making me stronger. Thanks to my dreams I had the opportunity to redirect my psychological navigational systems.

TWO

THE STATE OF THE STOREHOUSE

"I dream, therefore I exist." — AUGUST STRINDBERG

As soon as I knew that my dreams could be used to propel me toward the waking life I desired, I decided to research the subject of "dreaming" in greater detail (kind of like the way you only care to find out what a carburettor or a barium-meal really is when you think you might need one). Here's the nutshell version so you don't have to max your brain out with dozens of books on the subject as I did.

Right throughout history, from Far Ancient to Greek, Roman and Medieval times, and all those even more mysterious eras between, it was accepted that dreams tell us things about ourselves, about the gods, the world, and our past, present and future. A rather sweeping area of specialisation, I'm sure you'll agree. Dreams have been used to solve dilemmas, predict futures and to justify behaviours and decisions. According to sources like the Bible, and old plays, songs and paintings, it was quite commonplace for sleepers to be sent messages and visions. Teenagers in those days must have had an easy time, imploring their parents with claims like, "But the dream told me that I had to go to the solstice feast with Maximus-the-Mammoth, Son of Intoxicus the wine merchant." Of course, the parents could have countered with, "And my dream told me to sell my offspring to the temple of the virgins and eunuchs for the price of a yearling goat."

It is only since Enlightenment times and then Industrialisation that the power of the dream has become largely discounted. Throughout these last few centuries, logic and the conscious mind grew to be valued over anything as subjective as dreaming, which could be neither seen, measured nor quantified in any objective sense. Science was the new God and although some efforts were made to take a scientific look at dreaming and find its source within the brain, as a cultural phenomenon the dream lost its power. Of course, in non-industrially developed countries the dream state remained consistently revered, celebrated and educational.

In the Western world, post-modernism kicked in just in the nick of time. In the marginalised sectors of the arts, dreaming was prized as the basis of a purer truth bypassing the (corruptible or rigid) conscious mind, especially with groups such as the Surrealists. The drug-induced reveries of the 1960s revered all states of altered consciousness (not just the unconscious revealed but also the conscious mind distorted) and the boundaries between waking and sleeping could be blurred for days, perhaps years on end. Since then the dream has begun to regain its popularity.

For most people, their interest revolves around interpreting their dreams in a conscious way, working out what they "mean". Books on how to read your dreams are found on almost every publisher's list these days, lining the shelves of bookshops and libraries, not to mention standing guard by many a bedside in the event of you having a dream in which all your teeth fall out or you find yourself diving into a grain of silo with a mouse in your pocket. There's a pretty good chance that you'll encounter someone at a dinner party trotting out a morsel of wisdom in your direction, along the lines of: "Oh, you dreamt about a barking dog? A barking dog means aggression so you must be feeling really aggressive towards someone. It's funny, I thought you looked a little aggressive as you walked in, something around your eyes." You'll be left in no doubt as to who to vent that aggression on before going home to dream more specifically about killing amateur psychologists!

The word "dream" is also used synonymously for a hope for what will occur in the future, a goal or visionary ideal. People talk about making their

29

"dreams come true", and of "having a dream". This is probably because the images from night dreaming were the first places that people would unconsciously recreate their reality, where there were no firm barriers as to the way things could look and feel to a person. In Greek myth, people referred to voices speaking to them and visions appearing, as the idea of creating and imagining an alternate reality was not yet accepted as a norm. In times when consistency and survival were often synonymous, people would describe messages and visions coming to them in their dreams as a way of dissociating themselves from the messy task of igniting change or breaking away from the herd.

In the Bible Joseph talked of having a dream where his brothers would bow down to him. Now, imagine if he instead said, "I feel like I've been kicked around and ignored for too long and so my unconscious mind has come up with a great life-plan, the upshot of which will be me lording over the rest of you and sticking it to you for all the grief you've caused me of late." When you consider the ruckus that his (dissociated) dreams caused, it's just as well that he delivered his thoughts with the sweetener of them having little to do with him personally.

During times where survival was of the essence, it would have been harder to accept the seemingly selfish indulgence of having a higher calling or ambitions outside of your immediate circumstances. These days most people take personal responsibility for making their "life dreams" come true and now they can start to use their "night dreams" as part of this success, re-forging the link between the two understandings of the term "dream".

There is no common consensus as to the exact purpose of dreaming, nor can its physiological origins be pinpointed or its *modus operandi* precisely mapped. What we do know is that it is a random presentation to the conscious sleeping mind of things that exist within both the conscious and unconscious mind. When dreaming, images, sounds and sensations are experienced by the sleeping person and can be recalled on waking. (In a later chapter there is more about how to ensure you don't allow these recollections to fade so that you can remember them for long enough to New Dream.)

When you dream, images and sounds drift through the mind in a way that is mostly undirected and in a disjointed narrative. There are many hypotheses as to what dreaming is, including that it is a way of realigning signals from the pons area of the brain or from the forebrain; that it is a result of long-term memory; that dreams are random connections firing; or that they are mood regulators. No-one has yet proven exactly how dreams occur. Whatever dreams are, we know that you dream what you know, and that what you know makes up who you are. However, just as you do not need to have a handle on the intricacies of the stock market in order to successfully trade, and just as you do not need to be able to list every phyto-nutrient in an apple in order to eat a healthy diet, you can use your dreams to recondition your mind for greater success without understanding the neurological nature of dreams.

While there are some extremely skilled people who do wonderful healing work through interpreting dreams, many of us do not have the ability to read dream symbols. We are all, however, completely expert in knowing what feels good and what does not feel good in our own dreams. If the dog seems good to you, it probably is – it's probably a personal Lassie rather than a psychological pit-bull. There may be some argument here for the phenomenon of the "Universal Mind", a term popularised by Carl Jung, meaning that as humans we all share a common language of images and archetypes. However, you need to be able to identify subjectively whether the character in your dream is a Matriarch or a Wizard in order to use it as a diagnostic tool, and its usefulness is limited by the fact that it adds more steps into a very straightforward process of identifying what doesn't feel right and changing it to what works better for you at that time. Perhaps a character that some would see as evil or destructive might represent a more healthy "breaker of bonds" according to where you are at on your life's journey.

Everyone is wired up differently, so a dog for one

person could symbolise imminent harm; for another it might mean loyalty; while for someone else it could be pure freedom. Or your dream might simply be a reminder to get de-worming tablets from the vet. It's so important to trust your gut instinct when New Dreaming. If it feels good, leave it or enhance it. If it feels bad, what would you rather have in its place?

OVER TO YOU

Think of a dream you had either last night or at some time in the past. How did that dream make you feel? If you could change or enhance any aspects of that dream, what would they be? How does the dream feel with those changes made to it? Run that new version of the dream through your mind a couple of times, allowing yourself to feel better each time.

New Dreaming is best done immediately on waking, but for practice here (and because it may still be something you could benefit from dealing with), use an older dream. It might help to close your eyes and just quickly recollect the old dream without lingering on any details. Now start it at the beginning again, as if you were rerunning a movie. Take one aspect of the dream and change it, perhaps recasting one of the characters, changing the sounds or the colours, having people say different things, taking it into a beautiful landscape. . . . Allow yourself to breathe deeply as you do this, and enjoy the process. Think of it as you designing your life by stepping into your own dreamscape.

The Science of Sleep

What's all this dreaming business about anyway? It's doubtful that special dream fairies visit us nightly to sprinkle moon dust into out ears to produce dreams, so what do we know about where dreams come from and what their purpose might be?

We all have what is known as a "rational mind", and if the terms "rational" and "mind" don't go together easily for you, think of it as the mind that is aware of what's going on, the part of you that notices, enjoys, worries, works things out, makes decisions and creates. It's also known as the "conscious mind". Dreams come largely from a place beyond the conscious mind, a place known as the "unconscious mind". Easy enough for a primary-school student so far, and it remains so.

Dreams are images and sounds that are released from our unconscious mind during certain parts of the sleep cycles. Sometimes we are in a light sleep, sometimes a heavy sleep and sometimes in what is called "REM Sleep" where our bodies cannot move, except for our eyes, which flicker back and forth. Dreaming usually occurs during REM (Rapid Eye Movement) sleep, although there is new evidence to suggest that it might also occur during other stages of sleep.

So what is the unconscious mind, this place where our dreams come from? The unconscious mind is like a blank wall onto which all of our experiences are projected, whether we are aware of remembering them or not. Or you can think of it as "the storehouse", a phrase favoured by a guy called Milton Erickson who was to the unconscious mind what Einstein was to atom-splitting and bad hair days. According to Milton Erickson, the unconscious mind is a storehouse for everything that has ever happened in our lives, stockpiling everything we have ever heard, seen, felt, tasted or smelled, including all the values, emotions and beliefs we have ever experienced. It captures and absorbs every comment, every kiss, every snippet of news sent to it as well as everything in our vicinity that goes unrecorded by the rational or conscious mind.

It used to be thought that perhaps a dream is simply mixed-up images from the day before being released so that the mind can start afresh. However, it is now considered that other older stuff from the storehouse gets mixed up with the recently acquired images – known as "day residue" from the day before. Sigmund Freud believed that the day residue images were vehicles onto which thoughts from deeper in the unconscious attached themselves to be carried into the dream. Often it's the elements of a dream that seem bizarre or that you don't recognise which are the most important when it comes to making changes, as these are the bits over which our waking conscious mind has no control. Things have happened to us that we don't think we remember, but it is all recorded and is somewhere within, ready to help or hinder us in our lives. It's in there, so let's deal with it, making it bigger if it helps, smaller or gone if it doesn't help.

The reason that you New Dream on waking, rather than later in the day, is that when we are still feeling slightly groggy, still in that half-asleep mode, the path to the unconscious is still open. This transition period from sleeping to waking is called the "hypnopompic state" and is a perfect trance state, a state in which the conscious mind is not fully engaged so things can be absorbed on the unconscious level more easily. The brain waves behave differently at these times, allowing messages to be more deeply absorbed without interference from the conscious mind.

SOMETHING TO THINK ABOUT

The conscious rational mind is like a flashlight on the world, capturing everything within its beam, but that doesn't mean that everything outside does not exist except when we shine our light on it. We do not just pick up what our conscious mind focuses on, we absorb everything around us – the unlit as well as the lit – and it all goes into the storehouse. This explains why, under hypnosis, people can retrieve information they were not aware of having. During hypnosis, the stuff in the storehouse is let loose. This is often amazing stuff that the flashlight of your conscious mind never saw going in there, such as childhood family events or a number plate from a nearby parked car. This explains why people can sing songs they would claim to be barely able to hum and yet get them word- and note-perfect during stage hypnosis shows (although why people volunteer to go up on stage in the first place during those shows is still a complete mystery!).

We often have no idea what is going on in our own minds and therefore have little influence over it. For example, if we walk into a room and start to play with the cat, we might not be aware that we are simultaneously absorbing the mood of the person across the room, the sounds from kids playing outside and the smell of stale toast lingering from earlier in the day. There is so much more to us than the conscious mind could ever conceive and this has huge implications, both positive and negative. We have loads more great stuff in there than we ever knew, but also loads more nasty or un-useful stuff too.

Many people assume that the conscious mind can act like an automatic filter, that if you say to yourself: "Well, it's only a film" or "This war is happening hundreds of miles away", then you can block it out. Not so. The mind doesn't work that way. Our conscious minds may have managed to desensitise us on one level to all the news about war, violence and abuse, yet it's all being recorded by our unconscious minds. It's also worth noting that (given equal levels of emotion) the deeper mind does not differentiate between what is an imagined event and what is really happening to the person. Most people would not choose to physically live in a war zone and yet to all intents and purposes put themselves there nightly, having driven back to the safety of suburbia in order to do so.

My belief is that what goes into your storehouse is the making or unmaking of you. You want a cherry pie, put cherries in. You want a mud pie, put mud in. In this modern world it is easy to pick up discordant sounds, unhelpful ideas and negative emotions. Rather than being a case of becoming resigned to such phenomena and labelling it "reality", it is incumbent on us to increase our vigilance and ensure that far more helpful than unhelpful messages are recorded, as this becomes our default blueprint and ultimately dictates our actions and results in life.

Why is it that people who grow up in environments where money is made effortlessly, often go on to create abundance themselves? It's not (as is often presumed) the case that their parents gave them money or other unfair advantages; it's that they are imprinted with references, consciously and (more importantly) unconsciously gained, about the ease with which money can be created. Why then do some children of wealthy parents go on to live on hand-outs and in genteel poverty? This is because the messages they received were about being provided for and not having to work for what they have. Both sets of kids might have been given the same consciously absorbed lessons at school but what is unconsciously absorbed always has the most powerful hold; it always dictates the pervasive action taken on a routine basis. If you want to be healthier, take in messages that support health; if you want to feel at ease, avoid messages of strife; if your goal is long-term passion, then watching the soaps where everyone is freshly married by week three would not be the way to achieve this ambition. It would be wise not to underestimate how much rubbish passes for normality and goes inside us, slowing or halting our success and thus providing the cynical with more "evidence that life is not easy and dreams don't come true". You have been bombarded with unhelpful imprinting since birth, so take back control and refill your storehouse as if your life depended on it (which it does).

OVER TO YOU

What has been going into your storehouse over the last few years? Take a few minutes to write out some good and not-so-good things that might be getting into you – great or nasty smells, sights, sounds, textures, feelings, ideas. . . . These are the building materials of the self, and are the stuff that shows itself in your dreams. Even voice tones, textures of fabrics and other subtleties are sending constant messages to you about how friendly or hostile your universe is.

Take everything you have read over the past week – every paper, magazine, e-mail, website or book. Decide what percentage was:

Empowering _____ %
Useful _____ %
Not empowering _____ %
Slightly negative _____ %
Harmful _____ %

Some things might seem innocuous, such as news of a divorce, but keep in mind that you are travelling in the direction of everything you allow presence to, even though your conscious mind might be constantly tugging you away again. Other harmful materials would include a quick glance at an advertisement for a diet soda (full of harmful chemicals), a headline glimpsed about a so-called "credit crunch", or a photo where an editor is attempting to humiliate an actress or singer by showing her body to be less than perfect (thus sending you the message that falling short of physical perfection is wrong and that when you become successful in one area you will be punished in another – neither of which is true, of course).

Now voice-record your side of a typical conversation with a friend. Do you criticise or permit others to do so? Is your language supportive and enlightening or dull and uninspiring? Remember that you are not only talking to the other person, you are also sending your words into your own unconscious mind. What words are coming to you from the people you choose to spend time with?

Have a look around your living environment and ask yourself the question: "Does this area or object send in a good or a not-good message to my unconscious mind about who I am and what I am capable of being?" If you deem something to be neutral then it is in the not-good category, as it is failing to bring you to a higher place than the one you've been inhabiting for some time.

Now write out:

How can you cut off the supply of negative or unhelpful stuff? You might want to limit the amount of times a week you watch TV news, break contact with a certain person, control the negative phrases you say to yourself such as, "I just wish I could set up my own business" or, "How could I be so stupid!" Might it be a good idea to stop playing those predictive movies in your head about what might go wrong if you chose to start to make a big career change?

How can you increase the volume of great things?

41

You could plan your TV viewing so it includes mainly feel-good, inspiring shows, making sure that you encourage the people you know to have positive conversations through your example, or you could start incanting simple phrases such as "I can do anything", or "I'm happy, I'm healthy, I'm blessed", as you walk to work.

Opportunities are everywhere. Take action on three things right now that will, immediately and over time, clean up your storehouse. Notice how much lighter and more magical your dreams become after a few days of care over what you subject yourself to.

Often we send things into our mind that are contrary to what we want to experience in our lives. Perhaps we want to have a loving, trusting relationship, but years of certain novels, films and gossip from friends have stored us up with mistrust for the opposite sex. We want a quiet and peaceful life and yet we've been drip-feeding ourselves on a diet of violent computer games glimpsed peripherally from across the room as one of our teenagers absorbs the full hit. We claim to want to be financially free and yet we have spent years unwittingly absorbing the money worries of those around us. These worries might not even be spoken; they might be in the form of a facial expression or even just an energy.

One client complained to me about ongoing

disturbing dreams and was amazed when they disappeared soon after his computer game consul was consigned to the bin. This really is such simple stuff with such an enormous impact on our lives. Whatever we keep in the storehouse becomes our experience. We let it into the unconscious and then it shows up in our material reality. This is why so many people who focus on what it is they *don't* want are amazed when it keeps showing up over and over again.

Whatever is in the storehouse decides the state of our lives, and dreams are the best indication as to what's in there. Much of our behaviour, emotional make-up, and ultimately our destiny is decided at the unconscious level, so we need to roll up our sleeves and sort through this tangled mess of materials and decide what we want to keep and what we want to change. While we sleep we can spring-clean our lives. Dreaming is the more time-consuming pulling out of random images from deep inside; the New Dreaming is the stacking, polishing or chucking stage.

THREE

DESIGNING YOUR ULTIMATE DREAM

"If a little dreaming is dangerous, the cure for it is not to dream less, but to dream more, to dream all the time." — MARCEL PROUST, *Remembrance of Things Past*

When was the last time you walked into an estate agent's office or a car showroom and asked them for, "Oh, you know, anything . . ."? I'm guessing never. You're a little more discerning, right?

Before starting to sleep your way to success through New Dreaming, it's important to know exactly what you want from the process.

Next time you're at a dinner party or a table of people during your lunch break, take a moment to quiz your fellow-diners, ask them what they're ultimately aiming for, what their life plan is. I'd bet kittens on most of the answers being a little fuzzy, to say the least.

"I just want to be happy" is a big favourite. Great! But what will it take to make you happy and how will you know when you've got that?

The more practical might declare, "I want to be rich." Again, a wonderful aspiration. But how much money makes you rich and through which vehicles do you want it to arrive? It really is a vital question. What exactly do you want your life to be?

What do you want to achieve; who do you want to be around; how do you want to spend your days; what material things do you want; what range of emotions do you want to feel? And for those who claim that they just want to live in the moment and not worry about the future, I'd like to quote a couple of my favourite sayings: "If you don't have a plan for your future, someone else does" and "If you fail to plan, you plan to fail". None of us know what will happen in the future, so being as emotionally, physically, spiritually, financially and creatively fit as you can possibly be will ensure that you can weather any storm and thrive in times of abundance. In order to be at your best in the future, you need to decide now what type of person you want to be, who you want to have around you, what you want to learn and create.

Some people shy away from even considering how to make money but material stuff *does* matter. Those who say money doesn't interest them are usually doing so to protect themselves from the pain of admitting its importance and the realisation that they don't have it. Claiming to be more interested in "more important things" is a way of making sure they don't have to go through what they imagine would be the difficulties of bringing wealth into their lives.

The things we value most, such as family togetherness, health, recognition and contribution, are all so much easier when you have taken care of the money side of it. It's hard to feel good when your child is ill and you can't afford the best medical care. It's pretty tough to feel adventurous and free when you don't have a car in your driveway or a plane ticket in your back pocket. How will you feel when there's a seminar you want to attend but you can't come up with the cash to pay for your own ticket, let alone bring your loved ones with you? On the other hand, planning for money and money alone, will similarly guarantee disappointment.

So how do you get all the things you want? After all, you've been struggling hard enough for long enough and that Ferrari is not on the horizon and your mirror tells you that the Miss or Mr Universe pageant will not be calling you anytime soon. The reason is that you've simply been using strategies that don't work; you've been using only a part of your brain and using it in ways that create similarly small results each time.

Only when we send a specific message from our conscious to our unconscious mind on a regular basis does the magic really start to happen.

OVER TO YOU

Jot down three disappointing results you've been getting on a consistent basis as a result of doing and thinking the same way, and then write what successes you would like in place of those results. Example:

- I have been gaining an average of five pounds a year since graduation. I would prefer to sustain a toned, healthy body that is a good weight for my frame.
- I have been drinking a bottle of wine a day. I would prefer to only drink water and juice.
- I have been scraping by financially. I would prefer to build enough investments that I can comfortably retire in ten years or less.

Realise that what you have been doing is a result of the habits you acquired due to what has gone into your storehouse in the past. You can now start to feel good about those habits changing once you get clear on what you want and let your conscious and your unconscious mind know about it. You can start to dream big again, knowing that even though it may not have worked in the past, it can and will work this time because this time you are doing it differently.

Suppose one day, out of the blue, a loved one announced (paper bag in hand), "I'm going out right now to spend my entire life-savings on something interesting, but I'm not sure what." Most of us would plead with that person to give it more thought, to get more precise before they wind up with more useless doodads than a catalogue junkie. Dragging the misguided enthusiast back inside the house, you would probably explain the importance of getting clear on what would be the best thing to spend their life savings on, whether that be a buy-to-let apartment, stocks and shares, the development of intellectual properties or all of these. If you put some thought into how you want to spend money, doesn't it also make sense to get clear on how you want to spend your visit on this planet? A frightening number of people take more time to plan their annual vacation than they do to plan their entire life, and it shows!

OVER TO YOU

Right now is a great opportunity to kick back for an hour or so and have fun designing your ultimate life, using the suggestions below as a guideline. Remember, what you don't plan for will show up in some form anyway so you might as well have a say in it. Write up your vision in a nice journal and keep it in a place where you can easily refer to it.

DESIGN-A-LIFE

1. Love relationship. What specifically do you want to achieve in terms of a love relationship? This might be to have a passionate, honest and respectful relationship with someone who shares your love of helping others. You can then expand this vision and list the types of things you will do together and do for each other, the types of emotions you will regularly feel when you are around this person, the type of person you will need to be in order to attract them or continue to attract your soul mate. If you are already in a committed relationship, how would you like this partnership to develop? How would you like to take things to new levels and be even more excited about each other than before? What type of relationship do you *really* want?

2. Family. Okay, so most of us had no choice in the family we were given, but we do have a say in how we choose to interact with our extended family. What kind of relationships would you like to have with your family? Who would you like to be really close to; who would you like to be strong around; who would you like to influence? How would you like to spend time with your kids, parents and siblings? Design a typical day with your family, listing the activities, varieties of conversations and feelings you would most like to experience.

3. *Friends.* What standard of people do you choose to spend your life with? Our lives are a direct reflection of the people we associate most with on a regular basis. Write a list of all the people you know and would aspire to be like in some way. Now list the people you admire and still have to get to know. What traits do your ideal friends exhibit – honesty, determination, discipline, fun, caring? It's no crime to outgrow friends so don't feel you have to include certain people on your list just because you both played T-Birds or Pink Ladies in the school musical or whatever. It is also possible to see less of people, meeting up with them just once or twice a year. What type of friend would you like to be for others?

4. *Career.* What would you love, seriously love to spend every day doing? Forget about what you are trained in or what you have experience in – this is about what really juices you. It can even be something you haven't tried yet. Do you want to be the first commercial moon-rocket captain; president of your country; club DJ; inventor of a new beauty product; owner of a specialty sporting-goods store; religious minister; full-time super-parent; part-time property investor; healer; casino owner; furniture designer; dentist to the

dogs of Hollywood stars; TD? Really, dig deep here as perhaps your ideal career doesn't officially exist yet and it will be entirely up to you to define it.

5. *Health and Fitness.* What type of energy do you want to enjoy? How healthy would you like to be? What kind of health and fitness habits would you like to be part of your everyday life? What sports and dances would you like to try? How specifically would you like your body to look and feel? Who would you like to take on this journey with you?

6. *Creativity and Spirituality.* What space would you like to make for creativity and spirituality in your life? Would you like to create a piece of art, write a book, create a wonderful home, invent a new gadget, put your clothes together in a more interesting way, create a revolutionary new software package, cook a wonderful meal every week? Would you like to read more books by spiritual masters, spend time in quiet meditation every morning, take regular retreats, find a new church or integrate certain spiritual lessons into your life?

7. *Learning.* What books would you like to read, in which languages would you like to become proficient, what sporting or musical skills would you

like to master? How would you like to learn? Perhaps you would like to enrol in a college course, read books and listen to tapes or glean your wisdom personally at the fireside of an expert.

8. *Travel.* Where would you like to visit and what would you like to do there? Perhaps you would like to go to Egypt to see the pyramids; to Nashville to do some country-and-western singing; to Mongolia to ride horses; to Australia to lie on the beach all day and party all night. Maybe you want to visit places closer to you, the next town over, or a couple of counties away to see where your grandmother grew up.

9. *Money.* How much money will you need in order to live the life you have envisaged? Your money goal might be to have enough residual income flowing into your life that you never have to work another day unless you choose to, to be secure knowing that your family will never suffer because of lack of money. Once you have the gist of it written up, write a few pages on exactly how you want your financial empire to look, as this is an area where most people need more clarity. (You might want to get some books to help you with this vision.) Do you own an amazing business? Are you a whizz at dealing shares on-line? Are you highly paid by a particular company? Are you loving doing deals with people?

What value do you pour out so that the money can fast-track back to you?

10. *Contribution*. Who would you like to help and in what way? Would you like to finance the building and staffing of a new school in Africa or read to a child once a week in your local community? What are the small ways you would like to contribute to the world – by smiling at people, recycling, remembering people's birthdays? How will you know that you are making the world a better place? You can contribute massively through raising a caring and considerate family, or by being a role-model for your community. Think of what means a lot to you and use this as a jumping-off point when considering your gift to the world. If you are an avid reader you might find yourself motivated to help literacy, or if gardening interests you, then environment work might suit you better, or perhaps your love of talking can be used to raise important issues on radio shows. It's important to contribute in ways that excite you and that fit into the other key aspects of your life.

Take some time out at least once a week to review, update and expand on this vision. In order to achieve it, you must first conceive it.

Getting to the Ultimate Dream
through New Dreaming

Now you know what you want . . . because you have done the above exercise, right? If not, take the chance to give yourself a huge gift. If you don't have an hour in which to do it properly, at least take five minutes to get the basics down.

Now that you know what you want, you will be able to recognise those elements of your dreams that correspond to or are in opposition with where you want to end up. Perhaps you have a dream one night about owning a beautiful big house in the city but you have set a goal to own a big house by the sea – in that case you can New Dream that house with the ocean nearby. Perhaps you have a dream where you are in a room with a friend and you are just sitting around. If you are clear on your friendship goal, you can New Dream yourself and this friend having an animated conversation or partaking in some activity such as working out or cooking.

Samantha, one of my clients, had a dream where she was in an old bar with dark wooden steps. In the dream, Samantha was drunk and trying to get the attention of a (non-existent) woman she thought was more interesting than her, with whom she wanted to be friends. In the dream the woman ignored her completely and Samantha woke up feeling bad about the fact that she was drunk in the dream as she herself hadn't had a drink in almost a decade, having decided to give up her occasional beer for health reasons. She had set a goal recently that she wanted to pay off her mortgage in full by bringing in extra work on the weekends and was using most of her New Dreaming to achieve this end.

She kept her eyes closed and re-imagined the same bar, making it a bit brighter and herself completely calm, sober and happy. When the woman showed up, Samantha had her turn around and smile and then she passed her a business card. In the New Dream she explained to the woman about her goal to make a certain amount of money that month and the woman said she would call her soon as she had some work for her. Samantha then decided to New Dream it once more, again sober and again talking to the woman, but this time keeping the bar as dark as it had been in the old dream, as this simply felt right to her. New Dreaming is not about radically pushing and transforming everything, just about making the changes that feel right in the moment.

I met Karen after I had been speaking for a large group of people. She told me that she really wanted to give up her fifteen-a-day smoking habit. On these occasions I rarely get to spend as much time as I would like with each person, so I quickly explained to Karen how to New Dream, suggesting that in each New Dream, regardless of whether or not she was smoking in the dream, she would tell people about how much she loves being healthy and breathing fresh air, and that if cigarettes do show up, then to New Dream them into coloured sand, which blows away. I got an e-mail from Karen a couple of months later; not only had she not touched another cigarette, she had also joined the gym, was eating only live healthy foods and was now dreaming about health on a regular basis. Karen also used the pre-sleep programming methods which are outlined in a later chapter.

Remember when you used to write a letter to Santa? New Dreaming is just like doing that every morning. You've decided what you want by setting life goals, then an elf shows up (in dream form) and asks you if you want a Lego-set; when you New Dream, you say, "No thanks, I want a doll," or "Yes please, but a very big one," and that request is posted directly to where it can be processed so that it shows up in your stocking.

How does New Dreaming make it easier to achieve?

In Chapter One we looked at how the conscious and the unconscious mind need to be in sync for the creation of an empowering identity and consistent results, so that one part of you is not tugging against the other. But how exactly does New Dreaming bring them into alignment?

One helpful way is to think of the unconscious mind

as a large ship, and the conscious mind as the captain of that ship.

The captain (conscious mind) steers the ship, decides its direction, while the success of the journey largely depends on what kind of shape the ship (unconscious mind) is in. If the ship is laden down with tons of ridiculous and hazardous rubbish, it won't sail as efficiently as a ship that is carrying useful equipment and whatever is necessary for a fun trip.

Success also depends on the communication between the captain and the ship, in that it depends on the way the waking conscious brain and the unconscious storehouse are talking to and understanding each other.

As the captain, you are sending messages to the ship at all times; the ship is constantly picking up these intentional messages along with a whole load of other messages you are unaware have been sent. These might be messages from your shipmates (those around you), from the waters you are sailing through (your environment), indeed from anywhere in the atmosphere.

The ship also gets to send clear messages back to you, the captain, as you sleep. It sends them in a special "ship language" called dreams. When you New Dream, you (the captain) first get to look at what the ship has communicated about its understanding of the journey (you notice the dream). Next as the captain you get to correct any misinformation and send the desired details back in ship language (rerunning the new dream), so the ship can realign and travel along the intended course (directly to the required result). Without New Dreaming, all that you as captain can do is wonder at this strange language and get annoyed that you have ended up in Backwash Bay when you intended to sail towards Champagne Cove.

It's not really the captain's fault that he or she has been sending garbled messages to the ship; as we saw at the beginning of this chapter, many captains aren't even sure where they want to go and when headed vaguely for the tropics, it's easy to get blown off course. Even when the captain is sure of the desired destination, there is so much distorted information out there, ready to get soaked up by the ship. The importance of putting yourself in an atmosphere where there is as little distortion as possible is vital. Make sure you are around dolphins rather than sharks; calm seas with a brisk breeze rather than stormy or dead waters; around ships that are tending for the same destination.

ASK YOURSELF THESE QUESTIONS
Are you hanging around with people who favour your ultimate life or who fight against it (often for loving reasons)? Are you around over- or under-emotional people, in over- or under-charged atmospheres? Also ask yourself, are you able to follow other people, to model their behaviour to get to where you want to go, or is everyone heading in a different direction?

Working these things out will greatly help you to influence what your ship is absorbing. Life is not easy for any captain who finds themselves constantly having to steer against the current.

Often you are being sent far off-course, far away from your desired destination because of a strong or consistent message that was sent to your ship years ago, maybe even when you were a toddler.

Suppose your desired destination is to be fabulously rich. Your conscious mind (captain) may tell you that you believe you are a great wealth-builder and gives the command to build wealth. And yet, all kinds of non-supportive messages and memories from your past may mean that, on an unconscious level, you actually believe you are destined to live in a place of lack. You may now be commanding yourself to steer to starboard, while the "forgotten" memory of Aunt Ruth explaining to the three-year-old you that people with too much money go to hell, might be still telling the ship to turn to port. The unconscious mind (the ship) can't fully commit to one course when it has as many messages sending it to the "Land of Scraping By" as it has directing it to the "Land of Amazing Big Wealth". If you've never been very wealthy before, your ship might not even believe that the Land of Amazing Big Wealth exists and will not be at its most effective sailing to a land it doesn't really believe in.

This then subtly influences your actions and you remain half in a place of abundance and half in a place of lack. It's like driving with one foot on the accelerator and one foot on the brake – or, rather, at full-sail with the anchor trailing. You might open a brokerage account to keep money for trading shares one day and then fail to follow through with researching a stock. Some people call this self-sabotage, whereas really it is you trying to remain true to both the new stuff you are sending into your deeper mind and the old stuff that is still part of you. Nobody self-sabotages; we all do exactly what we need to do according to the state of our whole selves. That's why we need to keep the dialogue running freely between the surface and the deeper areas of the mind through New Dreaming. When the whole self is consistent, the message being sent is consistent, ensuring the action is consistent, ensuring the result is consistent.

The reason it is so hard to do this by simply sitting down and consciously thinking about it is that many of the messages we have been receiving are completely buried. You may remember Aunt Ruth only as a giver and inspirer, rather than someone who discouraged you from building wealth. Luckily, our dreams do the remembering for us.

REAL LIFE STORY TIME

A close friend of mine was trying to lose weight and my heart went out to her in her torment. She started the usual round of half-used gym fees; the daily walk with that determined look which the power-walkers share and dog-walkers lack; every food label read four times although she didn't know her kilojoules from her calories, even taking bark powders to loosen certain matter from certain places. This would carry on for a week and she'd even start to enjoy it, but then a phone call, a work situation or a great big nothing-at-all would cause her to revert to her old unhealthy ways. One evening, finding her with a half-eaten chow mein, an egg roll guilt complex and a king-sized Mars Bar threatening from the kitchen table, we settled in for a serious chat. I asked if food or weight ever came up in her dreams.

She said that she often had similar dreams around food and had dreamed one the previous weekend.

In the dream she was cycling along beside her sister. They pulled into a restaurant beside the seashore where their parents were eating. She then said there was a bit in the middle she couldn't remember but she did strongly remember that towards the end of the dream her father said to her, "It's all right love, you have to stay here." They then took her bike and the three of them went off to swim in the sea, leaving her with a full table of uneaten food which she knew she was expected to eat. When the waiter came over she was eating the food and she asked him if he did yoga.

My friend said that she had realised for the past few years that her father in particular had expected her to eat more and exercise less than her sister did and now she saw that the old expectation was still living on in her in some way, even though she was emotionally and intellectually past all that. She was one of the first people to whom I explained New Dreaming and she took to it effortlessly. Over the next few weeks she New Dreamed most mornings, running empowering new versions, whether or not they seemed to relate to body issues. Despite one slip backwards (possibly out of guilt over the lost revenue for the people at the Chinese restaurant) she found herself able to achieve and retain her ideal weight and level of health and fitness. She believes that if she had left the dreams as they were, she might have continued to slog against her own unconscious with each "failure" reinforcing the limiting messages held there.

My friend had always been good at remembering her dreams and before the night of the big chow mein chat, had often lain in bed in the morning trying to make sense of them, sometimes asking others later in the day what they thought they meant. Whenever we recall a dream in the ordinary way by just thinking back over it, we are sending that dream back to the unconscious in its original form. It doesn't make sense to send back the exact same message, that's like saying to the self that what was true before continues to be true, which

63

is never the case, as we are always learning and growing. And yet, how many times do we tell someone about an awful dream we had, essentially rerunning the same dream, reinforcing it in ourselves? In fact, we'll often send back a worse version as we exaggerate its awfulness for the entertainment of our listener. (People also do this with their horror stories from their waking life, a habit equally to be avoided.)

This is not about avoiding what is undesirable or what doesn't feel good, it is about using the bad feeling to signal that we need to change course and then changing that course immediately in our mind and body.

OVER TO YOU

After you have New Dreamed in the morning, share this New Dream with someone you trust, explaining first that you are sharing with them the new, improved version. What is it that makes you feel better about your New Dream? How can you change it so it will feel even better?

Since books such as *The Science of Getting Rich* by Wallace Wattles came out in the early part of the twentieth century, people have become aware of the importance of visualising what it is you want to achieve. When you visualise, you imprint on the Reticular Activating System (the part of your brain that filters information) exactly what it is you intend to realise. Once the brain has a strong impression of the required result, it becomes clear what action will be necessary and so the person starts to take that action. Lack of action is an indication of lack of clarity. When the brain doesn't have one distinct command, but has either no command or a jumble of conflicting commands, it will choose to do nothing, or simply do what is required for basic survival. When it is clear on where it is going, it will quickly work out the next step, and when the person is emotionally charged by the chosen destination, then they will automatically take that required step.

New Dreaming is a far more potent form of visualisation, because you are scrambling what you no longer want as well as clarifying what you do want, in a manner that is immediately and precisely pertinent to what is currently going on for you, and at a time when you are most hypnotically suggestible. In other words, you don't just get to ask for stuff, you also get to clear the path so the stuff gets to you faster, and your commands are louder and more definite. You'll notice that when you start to New Dream, you start to take massive and immediate action in many areas where you were idle or merely well-intentioned before.

FOUR

TOTAL RECALL: REMEMBERING DREAMS AND VISUALISATION

"Many's the long night when I've dreamed of cheese; toasted, mostly." — ROBERT LOUIS STEVENSON, *Treasure Island*

At this stage you have a clear idea of where it is you are heading and have started to establish better communication channels between you, the captain (consciousness), and your ship (the unconscious), enabling an earlier arrival at the desired destination. But what happens if you don't know what the ship was saying as you slept? What if you don't remember your dreams? What if you think you don't dream at all?

To the cappuccino-fuelled masses who feel that life is more of a racetrack than a treadmill, this may not be the best news, but the fact is that the body never really switches off. As we sleep, we also breathe (some of us a little too gratingly!), our hearts beat, we can digest food, repair cells and, of course, the mind is still ticking away in the form of dreams. Everyone dreams, every night. Even Mr Data, the android from *Star Trek: The*

Next Generation, had a dream program installed to enable him to share this human experience.

The degree to which we remember those dreams is what varies from person to person. Like with those embarrassing Christmas office-party moments, some people will totally remember every detail; others will have remembered and chosen to forget; others will think they remember but aren't sure; and others will spend forever wondering what happened (and were they naked?). Whether you need a little boost in remembering the details of your dreams or if you claim to never remember dreams, there are some really simple steps to get you to total Technicolor recall.

Having a comfortable sleep environment is very helpful. True, you could get great at remembering your dreams from under a nylon sheet on a sofa that is older than you are, in a smoky basement with Motley Crue playing all night overhead, but why do it the hard way? A comfortable bed and fresh linen, good ventilation, no disturbing noises, no disturbing wallpaper, and you're set. Another good idea is to stop eating at least two hours before you go to bed. The energy needed to digest food could be better used to remember your dreams. Drink a pint of water two hours before bedtime, as this way you are hydrated but not getting up to go to the bathroom halfway through an amazing opus featuring your favourite movie star.

Part Two of this book fully explains the best ways to ensure wonderful, restful sleep.

The next step is to give your mind a direct order as to what you would like it to do. Did you ever wake up just before the alarm on a day when there was something really vital to do? This is because your brain registered the importance of getting up at that time. You might even have said to someone, or to yourself, "I must get up on time tomorrow to do X," and your brain recorded and acted on this command.

For effectively recalling your dreams in order to New Dream them, say aloud to yourself before settling down for your nightly nap, "When I wake up in the morning I will remember my dreams clearly." Try to do this just as you start to nod off, as any instruction received between waking and sleeping (during what's known as the hypnogogic state), is more likely to be picked up and obeyed.

IMPORTANT! Every time you say, "I can never remember my dreams," you are sending a message to your brain to make that true. You are programming yourself to forget. So if you try this for one or two nights and still don't remember clearly what you were dreaming about, then do yourself a favour and refrain from declaring, "It still doesn't work, I still can't remember," as again this would send a command to your brain to ensure you remember to forget.

If you are the kind of person who jumps out of bed

69

first thing in the morning, singing and dancing and speeding for the juicer – and I know there are one or two of you out there – put a leash on it for a few minutes. When you wake up, remain in the same physical position as when you first open your eyes. If you do accidentally move, get back into that first-waking position straight away; this is because the body-position and the memory of the dream are powerfully linked.

If you really can't remember anything, that's fine. It may take a couple of nights of using the same techniques. Also, many people have their life set up so that they are required instantly to think of something else. If you wait until a baby wakes you with crying, set a gentle alarm to wake you at a time that is likely to be before the baby is awake and that way you can give your full attention to what you have been dreaming. All it takes is attention and everyone I have coached in this has managed to recall at least parts of their dreams after a week of practice. Try to start on a day when you can sleep in, as this allows you to drift in and out without having to switch your focus to anything practical outside of the bed.

Some people like to record their dreams in a journal or diary. When you do remember a dream, DO NOT reach for a dream journal to capture it, as this will just reinforce the old dream. Instead, begin to New Dream it immediately, to re-imagine it with empowering differences.

REAL LIFE STORY TIME

Former radio broadcaster Sinead swore blind that she had not dreamed since she was a small child, yet days after using these techniques, she was remembering her dreams vividly and New Dreaming them to great effect:

"I used to dream when I was five or six, and I was convinced that I hadn't had a dream since then. On Judy May's advice, I said to myself as I was drifting off to sleep, 'Sinead, you will dream and you will remember it all in the morning.' And I did! It was a crazy dream and I was so excited about remembering it that I completely forgot to New Dream it.

"The next night I had a dream about being in a room with my work colleagues and some people from my past. That was the most unexpected thing for me – that I dreamt about people I hadn't even thought about since childhood. As we all stood there, a huge fire started in loads of locations around the room, and I couldn't do anything or call for help. It was awful and when I awoke, I started off wishing I hadn't remembered it, but I realised it was still going on in there whether I remembered it or not. So I New Dreamed it. I left the same people in the same room, and this time when the fires broke out I called the fire brigade for help. Then I started to organise everyone and we put out the fires with foam extinguishers and buckets of water. When all the fires were out, everyone gave me a huge round of applause for saving the day. It felt brilliant.

"It's getting easier each time. I'm still remembering my dreams and New Dreaming them, and I feel that a part of me has opened up. It's really exciting to know that I'm influencing myself at all levels, and making my life better before I even set foot out of bed."

Another part of making it easier to remember your dream is to ensure that the temperature in your bedroom is comfortable for you. It's better to have the room slightly warmer than usual (not sauna levels) as this helps your muscles to relax. When you get good at recalling your dreams it is better to have your room slightly colder than usual as fresh air at night-time is vastly better for your health than a stale environment. Also, having a massage every week results in your body being relaxed enough for you to stay with your recent dream for long enough to New Dream it.

If you are still not finding it easy to remember your dreams after a week, have someone wake you up in the middle of the night and ask you what you have just been dreaming. However, for most people, just the intention of wanting to remember is enough to allow them recall at least the latest dream they had before waking. Some people recommend waking after every sleep cycle (every ninety minutes or so), but I have found that this leads to exhaustion during the day and so is rather counter-productive.

If only a snippet of the dream is available to you,

relax and New Dream that part, not worrying if the rest of the dream is a blur. Often, as you continue to relax, the whole dream will come rolling back. It's important to refrain from telling yourself, "Oh no, I've forgotten," as this is like sending yourself a direct command not to remember. You'll find, like Sinead, that with each morning your ability to recollect your dreams will grow stronger and stronger.

It could be the case that you remember the dream but then find it tricky to rerun the new version. I'm lucky in that imagining in a visual way comes as easily to me as dining and shopping. As far back as I can remember, I have always thought in pictures – very clear, focused, full-colour pictures at that. Whenever I daydream it always runs like a movie. I was shocked to discover, some time during my twenties, that some people don't produce pictures at all when they think, at least not ones they are conscious of. I was appalled and perplexed, because to me this meant that half the world, although having perfect external sight, was legally blind on the inside. My pity was swiftly put on hold when I learned that such people think richly in the form of words, sounds or feelings, and were probably starting up a collection for me because of the sensations I was missing.

Happily it is very easy to train yourself to think in a more visual way, so that running the New Dream like a film is easy. Equally, highly visual people can start to pay more attention to the sounds and words in the old and new versions of their dreams, as well as the feelings associated with them.

MAKING THE MOVIE: AN EXERCISE IN VISUALISING

The first step is to know that everyone can visualise. Without looking away from this page, say out loud the colour of the chair you are sitting in or the colour of the jacket or shoes you are wearing. In order to do this you need to have visualised them internally.

Here's how to get even slicker with it. Look at any object in the room you are in and after a few seconds close your eyes and remember its colour and shape. Open your eyes and check your internally visualized version of the object with the version in the room. Now close your eyes again and bring up the picture of the shape and colour and this time include other details such as the texture and size. Keep opening and closing your eyes until your closed-eye version is as clear or almost as clear as the open-eyed version.

Another fun exercise is to take a favourite old memory and run it as a film. If you need to first build up a still snapshot, that's great. Once you have your still snapshot, move on to the next snapshot of the event. Now run the snapshots more quickly in sequence. Pretty soon these will run together seamlessly.

REAL-LIFE STORY TIME

Gary was able to remember his dreams but found that when he started New Dreaming he was more likely to rerun the old dream – that the creation aspect wasn't coming to him as effortlessly as he wanted. The trick for him was to slow it right down to frame-by-frame, as if changing a photograph and then rerunning a speeded-up version once the new static images were firmly embedded. He found that this worked in another way as he carried around the "New Photo" in his head for much of the day.

Gary had a dream where he kept slamming his own young son's fingers in the drawer of a filing cabinet in his office at work. Obviously this was upsetting to him and when he started to New Dream it he found the child with his hands in the heavy metal drawer once again. Gery stopped the movie and focused on one still picture of his son sitting on the big comfortable chair behind the desk playing with the computer keyboard, Gary himself sitting at the far end of the desk and the filing cabinet made of pillows. He stayed on his newly created picture for a minute until it felt stronger than the old image. Once the scene was set in his mind, he then made it run slowly with his son walking over to the cabinet and taking out a toy before returning unharmed and laughing to the chair. Gary said that at breakfast time that same morning he felt relaxed towards his son rather than anxious around him, as he believed he would have been had he left the dream untouched.

When you are New Dreaming, the more precise your images, sounds and feelings, the clearer the message getting to the unconscious mind. If what really presses your happy buttons is the idea of owning a new sports car, really see the car when that particular New Dream comes about. See its colour, make, sound, smell, feel, with you behind the wheel driving and your ideal passenger beside you as part of the New Dreaming experience. Without any effort, you will find yourself being pulled toward having that car in your life. However, if you know all the details of the new sports car and yet leave the picture fuzzy, your unconscious mind doesn't get the full message and it will take much longer for it to turn up in your driveway. This is because the unconscious as well as the conscious mind needs to know what it is ultimately aiming for. With this information, it spends all its time making minute redirections in what needs to happen in order to achieve the goal.

Tonight, before you go to sleep, command your unconscious mind to wake you up at a particular time and to ensure you remember it. Have something different about your sleep space so that when you wake up you will be instantly reminded to New Dream – perhaps a brightly coloured cloth draped somewhere in your sight-line or sleeping at the other end of the bed. When you wake up, change just one thing about the dream to start with, or just one part of one image, changing a phrase, colour or object into something that feels better to you. Congratulate yourself for doing that much and build on it every day. Of course, most people can immediately start to recall their dreams and really get creative with changing them around – as New Dreaming comes naturally to the brain, it knows how to ask for what it really wants. You are already a genius at designing your life through changing your mind, and with practice you'll find yourself even more so.

Even if you do find it tricky at first, persevere! After a few attempts you'll be the Spielberg of New Dreaming, remembering your dreams and creating and running the new version automatically and smoothly. You are constantly designing your own life, so have fun keeping those designs exact and in focus, knowing that what you put in, you get out.

FIVE

UPPING THE POTENCY OF
YOUR NEW DREAM

"I've dreamt in my life dreams that have stayed with me ever after, and changed my ideas; they've gone through and through me, like wine through water, and altered the colour of my mind." — EMILY BRONTE

How quickly can you expect the New Dreaming to start taking effect in your life? You can *instantly* start to feel better, which is a great feat in itself, especially when you consider that most of our pursuits and purchases are directed towards that very result! The sensation of alignment between your desires and your reality is felt straight away and is wonderfully powerful and instantly inspires you to do more with your day. The fastest way to achieve a goal is to start to feel the amazing emotion you expect to feel once the thing is done, to get so excited and feel so proud and satisfied even before you take action. When you get this feeling going first, then the action will flow better and the result will be achieved effortlessly. If, on the other hand, you decide to wait and feel good only when you have the physical evidence of the achievement in front of you, you will take action in a more half-hearted, sluggish, bored way and it will be much tougher to get to that goal. So, even the initial great feeling you get from New Dreaming is speeding your vision towards you.

You want fast results; everyone does. Why wait to buy the dress or the sofa or the surfboard in a year when you can buy it today? After a few weeks of New Dreaming you may well be wondering why some parts of your life are changing almost instantly and other things are still taking their time. It would be wonderful if we could do a stock-check in the storehouse to find out exactly how much useful and un-useful stuff was piled up in there, but we can't. What we do know is that New Dreaming is speeding up the process of putting in the empowering ideas and images. It might well take a couple of years for you to move into that fantasy vacation home in the Caribbean, but at least it won't have taken twenty years. In any pursuit there is a gestation period where the material reality of the world needs to form in alliance with your thoughts, feelings and actions, and this does take time. However, the time is shortest when you play your part to the full. You can be certain that the process is working simply because the unconscious mind is absolutely incapable of ignoring what is sent into it and likewise the world is only able to conform to what is consistently asked of it.

I learned this in a very practical way when I caught

up with my best childhood friend, Tia, after losing touch with her during our twenties. When we finally found each other, in her adopted city of Paris, we spent hours in Café Flore drinking hot chocolate, filling in the intervening years as well as reminiscing about our time as hilariously self-absorbed teenagers. I was so happy for Tia; she had become fluent in French, made it to the top of her career in two famous international companies, married a cultured and gentle man, and spent weekends at their country chateau and summers on the yacht or in the apartment in the South of France.

"Oh my God, you must have stayed so focused," I marvelled.

"How do you mean?" she asked.

"Well, those were your exact ambitions when you were fourteen."

I so clearly remembered the discussions we used to have, usually when we felt rejected by certain people or frustrated at our adolescent state or were so lost in the hormonal soup that we didn't know what was going on. Tia was amazed. She had forgotten those goals years before and had thought her life was going in different directions, and yet here she had achieved everything she had set her (usually broken) young teenage heart on. (After that, between the ages of seventeen and twenty, the only goals we talked about were guy-goals, and these changed more often than the Irish weather.)

"And what about you?" Tia laughed. "You must have stuck to your plan like toffee." That idea startled me, as I'd gone from dancer, to director, to playwright, and had ended up in more jobs than the clumsiest witness-protection candidate.

"Your big ambition was to have a novel published, get some university degrees and travel by train across India," she smiled.

Wow, it was true. I had accidentally achieved all that. Those had been my reasons for living at fourteen, yet they were things I had lost interest in or given up on before leaving school. We then had fun matching our friends' lives with their teenage desires and seeing how successful we all were in spite of ourselves. Knowing what I know now about the unconscious mind, I'm not at all surprised that each of us ended up achieving what we did but I was also a little concerned that it could take so long to realise a desire.

Check in with the things you have achieved in your life without having paid much conscious attention to them.

Obviously life moves faster when you are no longer a teenager because you have greater means and freedom but the achievement of a desire taking more than a decade-and-a-half seems frighteningly archaic. These days, being used to hot food in less than two minutes and hot sex in under two dates, we expect all our goals to have similarly rapid response times.

Combining Existing Mind Technologies with New Dreaming

Before I started New Dreaming, I had already become skilled in many mind technologies that had been helping me achieve particular things in my life. I wondered if those technologies could be used to somehow supercharge my New Dreaming and help me become even more successful, more quickly. I soon realised that I had automatically been doing so already – that unconscious mind at work again!

I'd had a dream one night featuring neither plot nor people. There was a landscape with an old ruined building to my right, desolate faded-yellow grassland in the middle and a foggy area in front and to the left. In the dream, I kept running to the old ruin but kept ending up on the grass in the middle. The foggy area seemed too scary to even go towards. I knew instinctively that the ruin on my right represented my childhood, so when I New Dreamed it I turned this area into a beautiful fountain with flowers, animals and trees and slightly shifted its location so that it was still to the right but more behind me. The yellow grass stood for my present so I made this green and springy underfoot and peopled it with friends and supporters. However, after a few minutes I still hadn't managed to New Dream the future landscape in front and to the left, which remained foggy and barren. I seemed to have a case of New Dreamer's block.

Up until then, my point-of-view had been from one fixed position but now I jumped my inner-eye around so that I was standing way in the future, looking back onto the barren area. From here, it somehow felt much less threatening and I was able to create a beautiful patio full of people dancing, eating and laughing. Once I had this part New Dreamed I flew back towards the green grass of my present and turned back around again to look forward onto the future party. Just where the grass and the patio met, I sat down in a comfortable chair, feeling good with the past, present and future all spruced up and feeling no desire to run back to the past.

The mind technologies explain that all of us have a physical position where we locate our past, present and future. For many of us, we imagine the past as being located somewhere behind our physical body, the present somewhere around our body and the future somewhere in front of it. However, that is not always the case. For some people the past is located in front and down, with the future positioned above or vice versa. It could be that the past is diagonally up to the left and the future runs along a parallel line to the right. There are an infinite number of variations of angles and inclines along which peoples' past, present and future lives are internally mapped by them. You can use your imagination to move your idea of your past, present and future around so that it is positioned in a way that best serves you. It is considered preferable to have your past behind you but slightly to one side so that you can still access it when necessary. This is what I had done when I placed the fountain behind me and to the right.

It's best to have your future starting where your body is rather than a few feet in front of you, which is what I had done by sitting on the border between the grass and the patio. Flying out over your future, so that you can turn and look back over it, is another method which is used in Neuro Linguistic Programming. Neuro Linguistic Programming (NLP for short) is a mind technology developed by Richard Bandler and John Grinder in the 1970s that uses visualisation techniques in order to change how you think and feel. It might sound a bit complex, but it is in fact easy and fun and we do it all the time without realising it.

I was very excited when one of my clients demonstrated great natural skill with NLP, despite the fact that she had never heard of it.

REAL-LIFE STORY TIME

Catherine dreamed that she was in a dark, drab hall with a group of people. One man was threatening to kill them all if they didn't comply with his commands. His first order was for them to undress. Catherine did so, fearing greatly for the others who stayed clothed while simultaneously feeling great shame for being naked. She wanted to escape through the large double doors but felt there was no way out.

She woke up feeling terrible; but because she was in

the habit of New Dreaming she began to make changes and rerun the dream. She changed the decor so that the hall was brightly coloured and warm. Then, fully clothed and twice the height, she and the others stood up to the despot, whom she had now rendered black and white and blurred. He was instantly apologetic for his behaviour. With that, the double doors swung open wide and Catherine New Dreamed herself and the other people walking through the doors and out into a beautiful country landscape, leaving the tightness of the hall behind them.

In NLP, changing the submodalities (a fancy term for the brightness, distance, colour, volume, tone, panorama, etc.) of a scene is a way of changing how you feel about something. By turning up the brightness and colour in her dream, Catherine had made it a nicer place to be. Making herself and the others taller had given them more power, while making the man black-and-white and blurred had rendered him less powerful, less menacing. Likewise, going from a cramped to an open vista changed her feelings from those of being trapped to a feeling of freedom.

OVER TO YOU

The next time you New Dream, play around with the colours, sounds, focus, distance and other visual and auditory aspects of the scene. Notice which changes make you feel better.

Another self-help method I'd been using for years was that of incantations. As I run or I jump on my mini-trampoline, I repeat phrases that I want to have as part of my being. "I welcome my overflowing abundance, I welcome my overflowing love" has always been a favourite of mine. Any positive, rhythmic phrase such as "All I need is within me now", repeated over and over, is an incantation. An important feature of incantations is that the greater the positive emotion you feel at the time, the greater the impact of the phrase. The bigger the emotional kick you give it, the bigger the impact on your unconscious mind. So an incantation is a positive phrase that has the combined elements of (a) rhythm, (b) repetition, and (c) intensity of emotion. These factors ensure that the message is driven deep into your mind, so combining incantations with New Dreaming can make them stronger again.

In New Dreaming, turning up those great feelings to their absolute maximum ensures that the new version being sent to the unconscious is supercharged with great energy. It arrives louder, larger and with greater impact when travelling in on a super-emotion. Music is one way that you can get the emotion up to the maximum and add the element of rhythm. In any film, if there's music playing it's easy to get swept up in the emotion and the film is far more likely to stick with you than if there is no music and you only feel intellectually connected to the material. And of course, the more you repeat the New Dream, the more completely it becomes part of your conditioning. You can either use emotion, rhythm and repetition when New Dreaming as usual or you can even add the incanted phrases into the New Dream.

OVER TO YOU

Send your New Dream into your unconscious wrapped in a fantastic musical score (either imagined or with the help of a CD player by the bed) and feel the difference!

Take a phrase that you have added into your New Dream and repeat it over and over with increased great feelings. I have a friend whose favourite incantation is "If it's to be, it's up to me", and he now has himself say this any time he features in his own New Dreaming.

Even More Fun!

Being such a visual person, my absolute favourite self-help technique is Treasure Mapping. Once you know what you want in your life, you find photographs, pictures in magazines, sketches – any image of something that is part of what you want in your future. You then stick these images on to a piece of paper, including any extra words, quotes or decoration you feel is appropriate. This is your treasure map. It works by keeping you acutely focused on where you are going, a fixed aid to visualisation. I make treasure maps for different areas of my life: one for my love relationship, which has fun and passionate pictures of couples; one for my body, which has pictures of toned bodies and raw fruit and veg; one for lifestyle, with luxury items, etc. I have recently begun to draw or paint onto my treasure maps things I have New Dreamed, so if I have run a New Dream with me wearing a huge diamond ring, I will sketch that onto one of the treasure maps or find a picture of a similar ring in a magazine and stick it on. It also works the other way. For example, if I have a great picture of a little girl dancing in a ballet outfit on my family treasure map, I will put that little girl into an appropriate New Dream.

OVER TO YOU

Make or draw a treasure map, including all the great things you have been New Dreaming. This is a way to capture your New Dreams and keep them being fed into your mind each time you see them throughout the day. Like the way architecture is called frozen music, a treasure map is a beautifully frozen New Dream.

Another biggie in the world of self-help is the Attitude of Gratitude, focusing on what is already great so as to attract more of it and feel wonderful at the same time.

Fortunately, many of our dreams contain great things that we will have no desire to change. With these dreams we can show gratitude by New Dreaming them with exactly the same details or even enhancing those details, adding even more amazing feelings, music, making them even brighter and clearer. These great dreams really need to be celebrated as a sign that there is so much great stuff going on inside us all the time.

Unfortunately, the reverse is also true. You are likely to occasionally have bad dreams. In the next chapter, you'll learn how to turn these to your best advantage and use them to gain more restful nights and more peaceful days.

SIX

NO MORE NIGHTMARES

"I sometimes dream of devils. It's night, I'm in my room and suddenly there are devils everywhere . . . It's great fun. Oh, it takes my breath away."
— Fyodor Dostoevsky, *The Brothers Karamazov*

The books I read as a little girl frequently had a Victorian child waking up screaming from a nightmare and their parents or nanny rushing into the bedroom to comfort them and send for hot milk in a china cup. I would have made a hopeless Victorian hysteric, as my bad dreams have only ever made me open my eyes a little wider and spend ten minutes listening to my own breathing before falling back asleep. Even my worst nightmares would be hard pushed to earn as much as a PG rating.

Luckily, for those of us without day-to-day terror in our waking lives, those dreams where a twelve-foot demon chases you with a serrated butcher's knife through the sewers of what used to be your city are so rare that you might never experience one in all your 200,000 or so hours of sleeping throughout your lifetime.

However, the occasional uncomfortable dream can be expected. Some people do experience nightmares and these not only can be uncomfortable at the time but also can make the person nervous about falling asleep, spoiling what is one of life's great pleasures and adventures. No matter how bad your dreams have been in the past, this can be turned around when you realise that you have power over what goes into your mind so you can ensure that (sometimes immediately and sometimes after a short period of adjustment) only good things are coming out.

Now that you are a New Dreamer, rather than interpreting a nightmare as a purely negative experience, you can turn it into an opportunity to have a really good scrubbing-out of the parts of your unconscious that are sending such fascinating fare. Whenever I wake up after an uncomfortable dream, I'm really excited that the negative images and feelings have come to the surface where I can lose them and replace them with something better, rather than carrying such baggage inside me.

It's interesting that while having nightmares people typically sweat, getting rid of their body's physical toxins at the same time. You wouldn't want to put all those old toxins back inside you as soon as you've sweated them out, to lick up the sweat. No, you'd want to take a shower and freshen up. In the same way, it's vital that you New Dream as soon as you wake up from a nightmare. Often when people are in a bad mood in the morning, they are simply dragging an uncomfortable dream right across their day. So, even from the standpoint of not being a pain-in-the-ass, it's worth lancing the poison and washing it away. Often people spend ages reporting nightmares to psychiatrists and psychologists and feel little more than the relief of sharing the load, and often reinforcing the feeling by reliving it in its reporting. Instead, with New Dreaming you make a new choice about how you intend to feel from now on, releasing the old and moving on. Acknowledge what comes up, but don't bring it up in order to have it played out once again. The nightmare brings out the bad and you get to decide whether to leave it in that form or to change it into your new reality. As the self-development expert Tony Robbins likes to say, "The past does not equal the future, unless you let it."

Ask yourself whether you use the fact that you have bad dreams in order to get attention from others, or to feel connected to yourself, or to give yourself reasons why you don't have to step forward with your life. Many people love the attention they get from the person they share a bed with and this causes them to unconsciously create nightmares to fuel this sympathy. How much better would it be if you got attention, connection and certainty and variety of an amazing life through getting yourself to an empowered place of great dreams and greater New Dreams?

Some dreams are just mildly unpleasant. It might be just a glimpse of a three-legged robo-bunny that makes you feel anxious. Simply notice how the dream made you feel and ask yourself, "How would I rather feel?" Stay there until you think of images and feelings that you'd like to replace the unwanted feeling with. Robo-bunny now is a live bunny with all legs intact? Great. How can you make it feel even more wonderful?

Perhaps it was just one aspect of the dream that bothered you; for example, maybe the predominant colour was yellow and this made you feel despondent. Rather than deciding this must be because your mother made you wear that yellow sweater to your sixth birthday party and everyone laughed, simply ask yourself which colour would feel better. Would red make you feel more powerful? Or would white make you feel more certain? Perhaps just turning up the brightness and richness and making it a more golden yellow might do the job. There are no rules for this; your intuition will tell you how to turn a bad feeling into a good one or even into an outstanding one.

At certain times, your dreams may become more graphic and disturbing. In most cases this doesn't mean that you are severely traumatised or that your life has suddenly gone to Hell in a Honda; it's just the right time for this to happen. The whole of the mind is very protective of the person. You hear about people who have repressed memories for years until such a time as there is enough support and strength for the person to cope. Know that you can easily cope with whatever your dreams bring up and that you are fully in charge.

A well-known Irish artist, Sonya, has always suffered from terrible dreams whenever something really challenging happens in her life. During one stressful phase, she had a dream in which she was standing by the sea watching a bunch of penguins waddle around in endless circles, terrified as a huge alligator would jump up every now and then and snack on one of the hapless birds. Sonya stood there, powerless to do anything, watching the penguins waddle faster and the alligator drip blood from every tooth. At first she analysed her dream with her roommate and they agreed that it was about Sonya's fear that her friends and family were in real danger because they weren't taking any risks or doing anything to change their lives for the better. Although she came to an intellectual understanding of what the dream meant to her, she realised that she couldn't shift her perception of her friends and family and the dream continued to haunt her waking hours. She would be in the middle of a conversation or task or even relaxing at the end of the night, when the image would jump into her head, causing her to feel as terrible as the first time. After two weeks, she came to me for help and I suggested that she New Dream it, even though so much time had passed.

Lying on the floor of my office, she began to run the dream in her head, concentrating first on getting a good feeling going. As soon as she felt strong and peaceful, she threw a net over the alligator and removed it to a safer place. The penguins were no longer afraid and, knowing the coast was clear, clambered back to the ocean and swam away. What was interesting to me was that, had I been New Dreaming this scenario, I would have killed the alligator and had the penguins sun themselves on the rocks, but Sonya felt that her way was the best way, and she was absolutely right. It's about doing whatever feels great to you. Having run her New Dream a couple of times, she said she felt thoroughly relieved, back in control and free of unwanted responsibility. She even tested it by trying to resurrect it in its old form, but thankfully it had lost its hold completely and she continued to feel wonderful.

For Sonya, the dream had been revisiting her in her waking hours. Equally common is the dream that keeps coming back night after night, sometimes for years. An architect named Peter came to see me because he had been having a recurring nightmare for almost a year – at least twice a week, sometimes nightly. With his permission I taped our chat. Parts are edited for clarity.

PETER'S DREAM

Peter: I'm in my parents' house and I feel for some reason that I have to run to my neighbour for help. I come down from my bedroom and the main door is open, and I see a dark, evil figure. When I run from the house, I'm running as if in water so it's really slow.

Judy May: And how does that make you feel?

Peter: It's a desperate and a horrible fear, the pain of the worst thing I've ever had to face, and it's also exhilarating. What adds to my frustration is that it never really has an ending. All the time I'm just looking for help and the neighbours aren't in.

Judy May: How could you New Dream it? (I had already explained the concept of New Dreaming to him)

Peter: If I were friendlier to the person coming into the house, there wouldn't be a confrontation.

Judy May: Would they have to come in?

Peter: No. Yes. I don't know. Half of me wants them to come into the house, as if I'm comfortable with that. It's as if I don't know another way of doing it, it's as if I half-miss the nightmare if it doesn't come.

(This revelation had a huge impact on Peter and he looked shocked, and then confused.)

Judy May: Well, first, let's stop labelling it a nightmare, as that really just instructs you to feel bad about it. Let's call it an old dream. It's great that you've realised that you're comfortable with it; we are all comfortable with what we know, even if what we know is pain.

Peter: Yes, I can see that here (long pause), but I'd rather get comfortable with something else.

Judy May: That's easily done. How would you like the new version to look?

Peter: I want to keep it in my parents' house, as that's where it originated. I would stay in the house and not keep running away. I'd probably invite the figure in so it would be friendlier, I'd be in control. It already feels much better now and I know that if I don't want to talk to them I don't have to.

Judy May: It can often feel uneasy when you don't know what the person looks like.

Peter: I'd like it to be my uncle so it's much more friendly. He's passed on now and I always feel he's looking down at me. I don't need to run; I'm walking around the house with my uncle and talking to him, so I can keep the excitement in it. Usually I'm alone in the house, so I'd like to change it so my family is there, to have people around me. I'd like the neighbours who weren't around to help to now come around and see that I'm okay. In fact, I'd like Mrs Brennan to come around with an apple pie!

Judy May: You mentioned that it doesn't usually end. How would you like it to end?

Peter: I think there would be a party and then I'd leave with my uncle, who gives me a lift to the airport. We're laughing because he has the car that I want, a Jaguar. At the airport I get on a plane with my girlfriend Nicola and we fly to my home in France.

Judy May: So the next time you have this dream, which you possibly won't, run through the New Dream just as you did now.

Peter: I think it will be possible. I already feel that it can't just sneak up on me.

When he called me the following week, Peter let me know that the dream returned three nights later and was already less frightening than before, although he was still running from an unknown figure. As he was waking he said to Nicola that he'd had the dream again and she reminded him to lie there and New Dream it. So, keeping his eyes closed he did just that, changing some of the details from our discussion, this time having to answer the door and really persuade his uncle to come in. He also drove himself to the airport, leaving the uncle in the family home.

Four months later, Peter reported that the old dream had never returned after that morning. He also told me the news that he was leaving his job with the architect's office to go freelance, producing oil paintings of peoples' houses and large office buildings. He felt that getting rid of his nightmare had freed up his mental and physical energy to make this move. It also transpired that when he told Nicola the details of the New Dream, they began to discuss the possibility of moving to France as soon as her career permitted.

"And the Jaguar?" I asked.

"I'll keep New Dreaming that one!" Peter laughed.

You might find yourself having a dream where nothing is obviously wrong but it involves a person you don't want to deal with. In these instances it often seems easier to leave that person out of the New Dream, but it might be a good idea to change their role rather than replace the character. This is especially the case with ex-boyfriends, ex-girlfriends and former husbands and wives. You might be able to get them out of the apartment but there's nothing to stop them wandering into your dreams whenever you least expect them! But it's all for the best and even if you only consciously think of them when a certain football team loses or when it comes time to amend your Christmas card list, they will always be part of your unconscious mind.

One night I had a dream about a boyfriend I'd been with for a few years. In the dream he was selling newspapers at the side of the road and walked away with me to a café nearby. I felt totally oppressed and tied-down during the dream. It got worse as his friend joined us and none of us spoke; we just ate these tiny dishes of ice cream that I paid for. As soon as I woke up, I ran a New Dream and, saying goodbye to my ex at the side of the road, I was picked up by my new man in a sports car. My new man and I then went to a luxury penthouse suite for a party. However, as I New Dreamed the party I found myself looking out the window to reassure myself that my ex was okay.

It didn't feel right. So I began to New Dream it again, making my new man even more incredible, the party even more swinging . . . and yet I couldn't shake the bad feeling. With something as subjective as dreams and the unconscious mind, it's never a question of scientifically making a change from A to B and sleeping happily ever after. New Dreaming is more of an art, and as such often requires tinkering around with. Sometimes, like in this case, I find myself New Dreaming but then even the New Dream feels slightly uncomfortable.

Then I realised that it wasn't just about my making sure I was having a good time. I went back to the street of the old dream and this time had my ex-boyfriend met first by his (fictional at the time) wife and kids. I made sure they were really excited to see him and he obviously adored them. Only when they had left did I allow my man to come and get me in the super-car.

Over breakfast I thought about what had happened and had to admit that I had been feeling superior to my ex for years, assuming I was going on to better things and also feeling guilty for leaving him in the lesser place. It's hard to believe that you deserve something great, like an amazing new relationship, when you feel that you've done something bad to facilitate it. The New Dreaming also made me realize that almost a decade after we had broken up I was still associating those oppressed, guilty and bored feelings to being part of a couple. So it was no wonder that I had been pulling back from any long-term intimacy or going for unavailable men. In fact, although I'd been dating some lovely guys, in reality I was fast-tracking it to Singles Anonymous.

I felt completely freed-up that day and began to experience all manner of breakthroughs and realisations. I realised that the men I'd been attracted to had been very needy guilt-assuagers and I'd been ignoring the dependable types who were comfortable enough in themselves to just stand there. So I New Dreamed one last time, later in the day, and allowed my new man to just stand there silently at the side of the road. To my amazement, I still felt attracted to him and excited by him, as well as feeling wonderfully safe. He was enough, even without the sports car.

Don't get me wrong though. I didn't undream the sports car entirely, I just knew it wasn't totally necessary for my happiness. I believe every woman's storehouse should contain a convertible with her name on it!

OVER TO YOU

Look again at your maps of where you want to get to, your list of goals and your treasure maps. Take a few minutes to really enjoy the full picture of your ideal life, all your material possessions, all the activities you partake in, your amazing friends and family, your accomplishments and contributions and the full array of emotions that you are committed to feeling on a regular basis. What else could happen in your life that would make you feel thrilled to be alive?

SEVEN

HARNESSING THE POWER OF
THE UNIVERSE

"Even sleepers are workers and collaborators in what goes on in the Universe." — GREEK PHILOSOPHER HERACLITES

Everything in life starts as an idea and that idea is then grown in the universe by thoughts, feelings and action. Onward and outward to influence the whole macrocosm.

New Dreaming may at first seem to be a very insular exercise – one part of yourself talking to another part of yourself. In fact, that's only one element of the process. As well as the conscious and unconscious mind of the individual, there exists what's known as the universal consciousness or ground consciousness of which both are a part.

When you dream up an idea, this idea starts to take form and this form is either cancelled by a new thought or facilitated at a faster or slower pace according to the feelings associated with it and the type of action taken because of those feelings. So, let's suppose you intend to have a particular piece of furniture in your home –

say a rocking chair. First you think of the rocking chair and the idea is out there, the process has begun. If you do not really want the rocking chair or don't believe it to be possible, the weakness of the vibrations this sets in motion will ensure that no action is taken and the rocking chair doesn't appear, or that you take some action and give up before the operation is complete. Perhaps it is replaced with a new thought for a different type of chair.

Let's suppose instead that you have a lot of emotional intensity around the idea of owning a rocking chair and you take appropriate action; then the rocking chair comes to be in your home. It is not just happening on a material plane, however, as the idea, the emotions around the idea and the concomitant action all set in motion vibrations throughout the entire universe. (If this is sounding a little airy-fairy, please just stick with it for a moment.) When your own intention is vibrating at the same frequency as that which you desire to attract, it is magnetised to you at a cellular level. The fact that you wanted a rocking chair and went out and bought one is the outward mechanics of the process; the actual realisation of having it in your life first had to happen on a quantum level.

A thought is a form of energy. A feeling is thought with a specific and strong energy attached to it. Every thought and feeling you have affects the entire energy field of the universe. If you have the intention of being wealthy, putting out thoughts and feelings of being wealthy initiate real changes in the world, possibilities which you then reap through action. The energetic intention (or manifestation) sets into motion a chain of events which results in you attracting more money into your life.

Scientists are finally proving what many have known for centuries – that everything is linked. There have been experiments carried out where shrimp in a tank of water in one room react savagely when a plant in a separate room is cut. In another experiment, a piece of DNA in a lab is shown to expand and contract according to whether the person from whom it was taken (who is miles away) is being honest or dishonest. Everything is linked. New research shows that there are particles smaller than atoms that only take form when observed by us. The implications are huge, as this suggests that we are the creators of our own universe, originating from the most fundamental plane – that we are part of a oneness and can influence the whole, depending on how we feel and think.

With this in mind, it's easy to appreciate that the universal consciousness is a powerful force to tap into, a powerful ear in which to spill our desires, a point at which we set the process in motion. (Earlier we talked about Jung's archetypes as a part of this universal consciousness, but this is about the "one-ness" and not about the shared imagery of that same space.)

"Manifesting" is a process of purposefully putting out an intention into the world in order to bring about its actual appearance. Every time you have an idea, remember a need or say something, you are manifesting. "You brought it on yourself" was a favourite saying of one of the nuns who tried to educate me, and I have to admit that there is truth in the saying, both in terms of the good as well as the unfortunate things we evince in our lives. It's also possible to manifest something deliberately, to give it enough conscious focus and unconscious energy that it comes into being more quickly than it might have done. Under the drive of casual thought alone, it is possible to set the atoms of the universe vibrating in our favour. In manifesting, we set our goal vibrating in a way that the universe feels and so helps it to come about.

Okay, some of you might well be thinking, I get the New Dreaming stuff and how the conscious and unconscious mind work together, but this manifesting and universal hippy-drivel is too much. Yeah, I get that this is new to most of us and not what we have been brought up to understand, so I ask just that you keep an open mind and give it a go.

I have long identified with the idea that writing down a desire or a want, telling someone about it or sharing it with more than one person is a vital part of reaching the goal. However, I used to believe that it was a purely practical move, that when you write something down you are more likely to remember it or that perhaps you will find the note you made and be spurred on to victory once again. My belief was that telling people about a plan worked simply because it added a certain peer pressure to carry through with what you proclaimed. Now I know that declaring an intention, whether through incantations, writing up goals or talking to people, is also a way of harnessing the energy of the universe so it can act to bring about your goal more quickly.

It's not something that is simple to show on paper or to prove, but then neither is love, and we all know what a powerful force *that* is.

Trust me, talking about the energy of the universe is not something that would have happened a couple of years ago when I was still my no-nonsense *uber*-achiever self, but since first joining a manifesting group, I quickly came to see the magic of this practice. For about a year, every Monday at noon London time, five of us from all around the globe would manifest for each other. We each had detailed written descriptions of what the other four wanted in their lives and we would spend five minutes concentrating on each person. First, we would manifest for Kimberly, imagining her with her new family, her successful nutrition business, receiving an award for costume design, and so on. Then we would spend five minutes manifesting for me, the next five for Lisa, then Leanne, then Laurie. The effect of this global manifesting – seeing, hearing and feeling the goals as if already achieved – meant that many of the outcomes came to us far more quickly than was happening before we started manifesting. Leanne met and married her husband within the first year, I got a major book deal, Kimberly's nutrition business took off at a phenomenal rate, and there are many more wonderful examples. Dr Wayne Dyer's *Believe It and You'll See It* is one of many insightful books on the subject.

New Dreaming is in itself a form of manifesting and you can maximise the effect by launching the New Dreams further out into the universal consciousness. Tell someone about what you have just New Dreamed (leave out explanations of the old dream) and the blueprint is stamped once more onto the world, instructing the greater forces as to how you want it to be.

OVER TO YOU

You may find it useful to write up your New Dream in a journal, first jotting down the rough subject of the old dream, but keep this to one line, avoid going into detail and do not run it in your head. Next, describe the New Dream on paper in as much detail as you like, adding and changing bits as you go. Next, write what you learned about yourself in the process, again sticking to the positive side of the lesson.

These steps alone change the fabric of the thought and feeling patterns that create your world. You can then increase the speed of its appearing by taking the following steps. Write up one action that you feel encouraged to take as a result of this New Dream, and follow through. The action will be effortless because it is now more in line with both your conscious and unconscious mind.

Another idea might be to form a New Dreaming circle, meeting once a week to share your progress. Having a group of peers to keep you accountable and help you learn and grow is such a valuable asset in anyone's life. Most successful people have such a mentoring or support group to keep them on the upward track. It's handy to keep a copy of your regularly updated goals near your New Dreaming journal so that you can have fun monitoring your progress and can ensure (with the help of your group) that you're on the right upward path.

These days pretty much everyone is looking for new ways to keep one step ahead of the game, seeing gurus, therapists and counsellors, surrounding themselves with experts and advisers – all methods that show results. However, it's important to remember that all you need is already inside you and once you can get the ship and the captain sailing in the same direction, life becomes effortless. The great thing about New Dreaming is that it gets you to your outcome quickly, costs little time and no money. New Dreaming does the job of realigning your inner and outer selves so that you are free of conflict, free to create and enjoy the type of life that is right for you.

It's said that the first step to having the success you want is to get out of your own way. The next step is to decide on what you want and get rid of anything that is not in alignment with this. When you have identified what you really want, then a huge emotional energy is already in play. Believing that this outcome is for you then allows you to keep the energy building and ensures that you keep taking action, knowing that your success is guaranteed. New Dreaming facilitates all these steps, identifying and ridding yourself of what you don't want, identifying and ordering what you do want instead, keeping the channels open for its achievement, keeping the momentum growing. Congratulations on taking those steps through New Dreaming!

Now it's time to fill in the second half of the picture.

The next part of the book focuses on the more material aspects of sleeping your way to success – how to get the best night's sleep possible so that all the daytime and night-time activities are working at their optimum. Sleep better to play better.

PART TWO

IN MIND AND IN BODY

EIGHT

SLEEP MAGIC

"If you don't change your beliefs, your life will be like this forever. Is that good news?" — W SOMERSET MAUGHAM

In the first part of this book you discovered how to use your nightly dreams to radically accelerate the progress you make in your world – progress with your loved ones, your mission, your health, your riches, your discoveries and every other area of magic that blesses your life. You became a magician of the night.

Now, the next part of the adventure is the opportunity to discover a wealth of dynamic methods for ensuring the best possible night's sleep for maximum dream time and maximum repair time, alongside other strategies to support and inspire you as you sleep your way to success.

Question: How many times have you really wanted to take action on a particular goal but when it came time to step up to the mark, found that you didn't have the mental or physical energy to make it happen? The mental part of you was absolutely willing while the physical was slumped in that favourite chair.

"Later," your limbs promised the motivated part of you, "I'll do it later." And later became, "Tomorrow, absolutely tomorrow." And somehow tomorrow disappeared in amongst the dirty dishes and the credit card bills.

If only your body and mind had been firing simultaneously on all cylinders, perhaps you might now have that dream career instead of having another viewed cop-show under your belt. I know it's been hard in the past and it's probably hard right now, but it needn't be. Change can happen, and it can happen right now.

Becoming more successful requires developing the habits that ensure you have the vitality, alertness and animated vigour to match your dreams. Imagine a particular successful someone – a great parent, a famous actor, a powerful politician or even a superhero – and I bet the image you have includes that person exuding an extra measure of life force that sets them apart.

Now imagine yourself living your dream life, starring you as your best self as you move and interact and connect in superhero fashion, full of energy and vitality. We never see Superman yawning, dragging his ass and moaning that it would be easier if the city actually paid him for his efforts (unless, that is, he's been thoroughly whupped by a stash of kryptonite). It's all about having the energy to take action in a consistent and easy way. And for us mortals, where does this power come from? Sleep.

Good restful sleep is the superhero component that is missing in the lives of millions of frustrated people around the world. The right amount of quality sleep is the magic key to freeing you to achieve what you really want, and it's doable, no matter how hard you work, what your sleep history is or how many young kids you have at home.

If you even had one hour extra per day where you felt alert and on top form, that's 365 extra hours in a year or around two months of working days (working eight hours a day, Monday to Friday). Many people say that if only they had two months a year, they could bring all their great plans to fruition. Well, now you can! One extra hour per day is the very least you can expect from learning how to be a power sleeper.

It is estimated that half the people on the planet today have problems when it comes to getting a normal night's sleep. Sadly, the solution for many is to self-medicate themselves into a comatose state that is less than restorative; or alternately they may put up with a nightly dance of twisting and turning in sweaty sheets. Thankfully, sleep, like other skills, can be learned and improved upon.

It must be noted at this point that some sleep problems can have their basis in a developing illness, so please visit your doctor to ensure that this is not the case with you.

Beliefs

As we discussed in Part One, what you believe about yourself as an individual influences what happens to you. Actions you take and fail to take are consistent with your beliefs.

This also holds true for your beliefs and identity around sleep. If you believe yourself generally to be a sound sleeper, you are not likely to get freaked out if you spend a couple of nights of fitful rest due to something you have on your mind. Similarly, if you believe yourself to be a "bad sleeper" then you're likely to write off a month of good sleep as a fluke or a tease and you will probably not try any new techniques, thinking that yours is a hopeless case. Your belief in your ability to improve the quality (and quantity if necessary) of the sleep that you get determines how successful your sleeping outcome will be.

SELF-EXPLORATION

What do you believe about yourself as a sleeper?

- I'm a great sleeper – I can nod off anywhere
- I'm a restless sleeper, waking a couple of times during the night
- I'm a complete insomniac
- Sleep is for sissies
- Sleep is my favourite thing in the world

- I sleep too much
- I sleep too little
- I'll sleep when I'm dead
- If I sleep too long I'll miss something
- Sleep is vital to my health and happiness
- Sleep is something I never have time for
- Sleep is just sleep
- Sleep is something that others do better than I do
- Other . . .

Your beliefs are made up of evidence you have collected in the recent or distant past. Perhaps you overheard a parent during your childhood say that you slept soundly all night, or perhaps at one time in your life you had trouble nodding off for a few nights in succession and decided that you were a bad sleeper. You might have made the link between "sleep" and "feeling good" or you might have made a link between "sleep" and "feeling bad". You may have lots of evidence that seems to support your belief but the good news is that if this belief is not fully supporting you in getting the finest possible sleep, then it can be changed quickly and easily.

Simply by deciding instead to believe, "I am a fantastic sleeper who gets good, healing rest throughout the night" or even "I can learn to be a fantastic sleeper" or "I can learn to manifest all my desires as I sleep", you are well along the path to creating new evidence to support that belief.

If you retain the unhelpful beliefs with labels attached such as "I am an insomniac", then you are far less likely to do what it takes to become a better sleeper. As humans we always consciously and unconsciously do whatever it takes to stay consistent with our beliefs and our identity for ourselves.

Remember, there is NO right and wrong way to sleep, just some ways that serve you better than others.

Daytime beliefs also impact your night-time success. If your identity and the value you see in yourself is that of "hard worker", then being exhausted all the time will allow you to feel superior to those who get enough rest. The downside is that your intimate relationship, your health and your efficiency all suffer and you don't get to ever really feel good, just pumped up on this notion that you're "making it happen".

What has been your major belief about yourself as a sleeper up until today?

My old belief about myself as a sleeper is _____

What new, better belief do you now intend to have about yourself as a sleeper?

My new, more empowering belief about myself as a sleeper is _____

Being a "bad" sleeper can meet many of your needs. You can get attention and sympathy from the people close to you and you don't have to follow through on your plans because you have the excuse of being tired. There is always a reason for retaining an unhelpful situation; we call this a "secondary gain". Could it be that if you were to feel fully rested then you would have to take action to change your life? Could it be that if you had the energy you might then have to focus on your finances or your relationship? Would there be intimate expectations of you such as sex or personal conversation if you didn't have the excuse of being exhausted? Do you feel relieved to be able to blame someone for your lack of sleep because you are angry, and yet can't face holding yourself or someone else responsible for a far more destructive personal situation? The more you protest against these possibilities, the more important it is to get really honest with yourself. There are reasons why we do everything, including the way we sleep.

OVER TO YOU

Write up some notes on the following, aiming for at least three ideas for each question.

- How has being an unsuccessful sleeper met your needs in the past? (Maybe it has brought you closer to someone you like or further away from someone who repels you; or it has mixed things up and kept them interesting; or it has made you feel important, made you feel safe in ways that feel familiar to you; or it has allowed you to do fun things instead like dancing or connecting to people.)

- How will being a successful sleeper in the future meet your needs in a much better way?

- How will being a successful sleeper change your life for the better?

When it comes to making changes, we are all veritable geniuses at making excuses as to why we have stayed in the old place. Unfortunately, excuses don't get you any farther down the road; they just keep you treading water. It's time to throw out all the excuses you've been using and to come up with solutions that will help you to become a better sleeper.

OLD EXCUSE	SOLUTION
I have three kids who wake up at six	Go to bed earlier, make more time by getting older kids to help with chores.
I have a very demanding job	Recognise that there is a point beyond which activity is not producing results.
I have always needed medication	Go to your doctor and find a way to reduce your meds; look into natural alternatives.
I don't have enough money to make my room comfortable	Use soap and water, rearrange the furniture, borrow some cushions.

If you argue for your limitations, they are yours to keep.

What have been your old sleep excuses until now and what solutions can you apply immediately?

NOTE: Although many get less sleep than they ideally need, some people sleep too much, staying in bed after ten or twelve hours of sleep, and then continue to nap during the day. Unless you are recovering from an illness or this occurs after days or weeks of sleep deprivation, you need to see your doctor. Over-sleeping is one of the fundamental signs of depression. Ensure you are given help beyond a prescription; you need to find a way to get excited and motivated about your life. A good way to start is by looking at some of the suggested readings at the back of this book. If someone you know is sleeping strange hours and sleeping a lot, you must heed this warning sign, even if they insist that everything is fine. Over-sleeping is not normal for anyone, whether they are a student, in mourning, a young man, unemployed, a teenager or from any other group. Anyone sleeping too much must get professional help immediately.

Set your Sleep Clock

Going to bed at the same time every night and getting up at the same time every morning is the best strategy for feeling lively and active throughout the day. Decide how many hours you would like to sleep, from what time to what time, and start tonight to sleep for that duration, even if you are lying awake ceiling-staring periodically for the first few nights. Give yourself permission to go to sleep instead of telling yourself lies such as I "ought" to be working or I "should" spend more time tidying the living room.

Wake up and get up (after New Dreaming) at your desired time in the morning, accepting that you might be exhausted for the first couple of days into your new sleep routine, but soon it will start to feel effortless. Most people function best on between seven and nine hours' sleep. Although modern myth would have us believe that six hours a night is possible, this is not something to aspire to, as it actually costs you time in terms of efficiency and health. Going without sleep is simply not an option; sleep is a matter of life and death. The National Highway Traffic Safety Administration says that over 1,500 deaths are caused in America each year by driver fatigue, while in Ireland the National Safety Council has said that up to one-in-five road accident deaths are fatigue-related. Countless more accidents occur in the workplace and at home simply because people hadn't organised their lives in such a way that it is standard procedure to get enough sleep. This lack of organising our lives so that we get sleep is unusual when you consider how well we tend to take care of other basics such as the need for fluids and food.

The body works on cycles and rhythms and the sleep cycle can take a few days to set. Sticking to that cycle is paramount to sleeping successfully, so on the weekend ensure that you do not go to bed too long after your usual bedtime and try not to sleep in for too long either. If you miss out on some sleep one night, due to a sick child or wild party or a late-night telethon where Ryan Tubridy might appear, you might like to catnap later in the day.

Many people feel that getting up out of bed in the morning is the toughest thing they do in the average day. This may be because they have not gone to bed eight or seven-and-a-half hours before they need to be awake, but often it is because they have set up their lives so that they have no reason to want to get up. Lying there is a better option than what is on the immediate horizon. "Okay," the brain says, "I can either snuggle down and snooze some more or get up and put the garbage out and then put on that cheap scratchy suit and sit snarled up in traffic on the way to that boring job. Hhmmm, let me see . . ." Not much of a contest, is it?

The trick is to make sure that outside-the-bed feels as good as (or better than) inside-the-bed, and that usually means getting up to do something that you really love. Remember how, as a child, you used to bounce into action on the first morning of the summer holidays, or when you knew there were gifts waiting for you downstairs, or when there was snow on the ground, or just because you knew there would be some fun or trouble going on somewhere? If your favourite film star was sitting in your kitchen waiting for you to prepare some fresh orange juice for them, you'd feel slightly motivated to get up and at least find out if they wanted toast with that. If you were told that every morning there would be a fifty euro note on the kitchen floor for you to pick up, but it would only be there between 6.30 and 6.45, would that be enough for you to reach for your dressing gown and trot downstairs?

Unfortunately, many of us have organised (or failed to organise) our mornings in such a way that we are engaged in dull or stressful activities from the off. New Dreaming will already have helped you with this challenge, as you will feel terrific from rearranging your truth and your vision, but what about after that? How strong or weak is the temptation to pull the covers back over your face and catch another ten minutes' shut-eye?

Getting up with gusto trains your body to be either awake and energised or sleeping deeply; none of this "sluggish days" and "fitful nights" business anymore. The more you use your body in ways that are dynamic and powerful during the day, the better you will sleep at night, consequently the more refreshed you will feel and so be able to use your body in dynamic and powerful ways during the day, and so the better you will sleep . . . and so on.

Suggestions for Feeling Good on Waking and Getting up

The night before:

Get excited about the next day; think of it as party time and have fun preparing. The night before, have the kitchen clean and the breakfast things laid out, and have all lunches prepared and bags packed. What can you do to give it that extra boost? A picnic breakfast on the living-room floor, or a note in someone's lunchbox, or a huge bunch of flowers to greet you when you come downstairs, or all your workout gear laid out with your favourite inspirational speaker ready on the DVD player.

It's important to choose in advance the music or motivational materials you are going to play in the morning; avoid the radio and TV because with these media other people get to dictate your mood and what goes into your storehouse and it's usually superficial or stressful stuff that will end up being filed. Be in charge from the moment you wake up; it feels better.

The morning time:

- Parents – get up an hour before your kids and enjoy a quiet, relaxed breakfast together. Yes, many parents of young kids do this, it *is* possible.

- Plan a really delicious breakfast of your favourite healthy foods.

127

- Set the heating or air-conditioning systems in such a way as it will be warm or cool enough to be comfortable from the moment you wake.

- Fix a stimulating business meeting or conference call – one that you can't cancel – for soon after you get up.

- If you are reading a tantalising book that you can't put down, one where you simply must find out who seduced the miller's daughter, go to sleep and get up an hour earlier and read it only in the morning.

- Find a way to be doing a job that you absolutely adore so that you leap out of bed with excitement thinking about what will happen that day.

- Have a special journal or notebook where you write up your plans for the day and all the wonderful things you are going to achieve. You might even do this before you go asleep so that you can focus on it as soon as you've finished New Dreaming.

- Watch half an hour of a great uplifting movie each morning as you eat breakfast, either more serious fare such as *Master and Commander*, or fun stuff like *The Sound of Music*.

- Arrange to gather with friends for breakfast or organise a breakfast club where you and your friends or colleagues (and perhaps all your kids) meet to motivate each other for the day ahead. You can do this once or twice a week if daily is too much of an undertaking.

- Go for a gentle dawn walk.

- What is your favourite hobby? Flower arranging, collecting autographs, playing tennis, writing music, cooking, mountain biking, playing cards? Whatever it is, schedule to get up an hour earlier than usual to get some fun racked up before work starts.

- Arrange to meet your lover in the shower or jacuzzi.

- If you have tried and failed at the early-morning-run routine, go for different early morning ways to move: skating, horse-riding, bike-riding, dancing, or something else that feels more like a prize than a punishment.

- Paint a picture, paint the patio or take photographs of the dawn.

- Listen to a motivational self-help CD.

- Write your book. Many famous first novels were conceived and created at the kitchen table before the rest of the household awoke.

- Get online and trade some stocks.

- Get a massage or have another beauty or fitness expert call to your door.

- Talk to your mother on the phone.
- Make something: a rocket, or some muffins, a shelving unit, an outfit or a new game.

If just the physical act of getting out of bed is the tough part; if you could sleep through a battalion of construction workers beneath your window, never mind a simple alarm clock; if you press the snooze button so often your thumb has a permanent indent, here are some ideas for you:

- Set three or four alarm clocks to go off all around the house, so you have to get up and move to switch them off.
- Set an electrical timer to turn on a fan to blast cold air in your direction.
- Arrange for a friend to call you at your wake-up time and perhaps calling you back five minutes later, after you have done your New Dreaming, to make sure you are up and about.
- Borrow a very young child or a dog!

When you get up to do a fun activity, you might then find yourself tempted to switch to doing something more mundane and "necessary" such as the laundry or vacuuming or something else that simply "must get done". Avoid this temptation and stick to the fun choice, as otherwise your brain will start to disbelieve you that it's worth getting up and you'll start to sleep in again. It is vital to train yourself so that both going to sleep and getting up are pure pleasure.

We have become so conditioned to believe that we need to go straight to work or school as soon as possible after waking, with maybe a fast shower and a cereal bar grabbed along the way. Every TV show that depicts a morning-scene has people rushing and sniping and clamouring and fighting. Who says it needs to be this way?

ANSWER THESE QUESTIONS:

- What is your new belief about how your morning can be?

- What will you do right now to make that happen?

- How much easier will it be to wake up to that ideal morning every day?

In some cases, travel commitments make it harder at times to keep to the same sleep cycle. With cheaper flights and so much international business being done in person, more people than ever travel across time zones on a regular basis. This messes with your body clock but needn't spell disaster. The trick is, if you are scheduled to be there for more than two days, to get yourself acclimatised to the time zone of the place you have arrived in as soon as possible, change your watch or clock to the local time on landing and substitute lost hours with short one-hour naps during the day. Some people find taking anti-jetlag treatments are helpful (such as Menatonin, which helps reset the body clock) and others find that just letting yourself go through the drowsy-by-day, awake-at-night routine for a couple of days does the job. The next time your sleep patterns are interrupted by travel or shift-work, keep a diary of what happens and what helps and hinders the situation, so that you can actively make plans for the next time.

The same common-sense approach is needed when it comes to taking naps during an average day. Restrict your nap to less than an hour and ensure that regular naps do not disrupt your sleep cycle. Ask yourself how you feel after you nap – better or worse? Is there usually something that has just happened or something that is about to happen when you feel the urge to nap? Are you bored or wanting to avoid something? Are you sleepy because you have just eaten a large meal with empty calories? In this case it might be more advisable to re-invigorate yourself with a brisk walk in the open air. If working in a busy office makes napping difficult (although many offices would have a spare conference room you could slip into for twenty minutes during your lunch break), the fresh-air option might be an easier one.

Sleep Disorders

The phrase "sleep disorders" is just shorthand that the scientific profession uses to put in one box the ways in which people sleep differently from what might be considered the norm. This may be helpful in working out what needs to be made better but unfortunately many people slap on a term and wear it like an identity badge and an excuse for remaining where they are at. Please remember that the "sleep disorder" industry is worth billions of euros and if you want to avoid paying into that machine, realise that there are many different ways of getting a better night's sleep which you can achieve easily, tonight and without professional intervention. I must emphasise again at this point that sometimes there is a medical reason for lack of sleep, such as iron deficiency and diabetes causing restless leg syndrome, so make sure you go for a check-up to discover if you need medical treatment. There are also very rare cases of people who have conditions such as narcolepsy (constant falling asleep), and although these are outside the scope of this book, the content here can also be of help to those with such conditions. Once again, check with your physician. However the vast majority of sleep disturbance can be easily rectified through finding new sleep strategies such as those in this book.

For most people, sleeplessness has more to do with habits and beliefs than with your biochemistry. This book does not assume that there is anything wrong with you. No matter what your starting point is, you can get more and more proficient at sleeping in the way you would ideally choose. If you are alive and reading this book, then you have been getting enough sleep; now perhaps you'd like to get some more so that you can feel even better.

You can get the kind of sleep you want by making a few changes to the way you think and feel and the things you do. If this belief bothers you, it might be worthwhile looking at what you are gaining by believing that yours is a difficult case. Does it make you feel special and different to be a troubled sleeper or "insomniac"; does it mean you can avoid or partake in certain things; is it just what you've always believed; or do you believe that it's time for things to change and that you can and will change them immediately?

The biggest complaint from people is that they have trouble sleeping right the way through the night. They grace it with the name "insomnia" but really it's just a state of being awake when you would expect and prefer to be asleep. Granted, it can be immensely frustrating, but if you continue to do what you've been doing, then you'll get the same result. It's time to try something new. The trick here is, instead of trying to sleep, focus on having the most blissful and most restful awake-at-night time that you possibly can.

When you were younger and at a slumber party or

it was Christmas Eve and you couldn't sleep, remember how happy and excited you were. Here was the chance to make hot chocolate, talk with your friends or siblings, enjoy the feeling of walking round the house when no one else could see you. Remember how you giggled and rushed from one room to another? Perhaps being awake when others are asleep has lost its novelty value for you. How can you get that feeling back? What fun stuff can you do during this magical awake-at-night time?

I often advise people who claim they can't sleep to remember a time when they loved sleeping and then recreate that for one night. This breaks the pattern of sleeplessness, as you can't follow the same thought patterns and behaviour patterns that have been contributing to your restlessness.

Here are some examples of great sleep events shared by many:

- In a tent in the back garden.

- A romantic night in a hotel room.

- With a large flashlight and an adventure book to read under the covers.

- In sleeping bags with friends in the living room.

- In a hammock or on a lounger by the beach.

- With all your childhood soft toys in bed with you.

- Watching *ET* with a cup of hot milk on a sofa bed in the living room.

• On a blanket under a "fort" you have made with the living room furniture.

• On a sleeper bunk in a train speeding across Europe.

Yes, it's simple and, yes, it works.

Most people who claim to be insomniacs get their sleep during the day in naps, or they try one sleep strategy and then another, rarely using all the tools at once.

Here's a quick checklist:

1. No caffeine or sugar at all during the day.

2. Go to bed and get up at the same time for a week.

3. Ensure your sleep environment is as good as it can be (next chapter).

4. Ensure your have given yourself enough time to wind down.

In fact, in order to not be an "insomniac", you need to do all the things explained in this half of the book. The successful sleepers are not "lucky"; they are just doing many of the things needed without knowing they are doing them.

If I ever have trouble sleeping, which is usually after a long-distance flight, I get up and cook a healthy meal. The repetitive actions of chopping and stirring keep me from feeling bored and yet don't over-stimulate my mind. The next morning I then put the meal in the fridge or freezer. I once spoke to a man at an airport who told me that he learned to knit in order to fill the odd waking hour. When your awake-at-night time is productive, you are far less likely to feel resentful about it. If you find yourself awake in bed for more than twenty minutes, turn your alarm clock to the wall so that you can't do a countdown of all the sleep you're not getting, get up out of bed and do something positive and restful for half an hour, and then get back to bed. Ensure you still get up at your routine time, so that you will be better able to sleep the following night.

The bad feelings many people get from being unable to sleep in exactly the way they want and for the time period that they desire comes from the judgement they have about the fact that they are not asleep. They allow themselves to get annoyed, weepy, angry, frustrated, overwhelmed, and so on, because they have beliefs such as:

- This means that I will feel awful tomorrow.

- I'm such a failure – everyone else is asleep.

- If I don't fall asleep now I won't get any sleep at all tonight.

- It's not fair, this always happens to me.

Why not allow the time you are not asleep to trigger great feelings of excitement, calm, connection to God, reflection, creativity . . . ? This is easily achieved by attaching great meanings to the waking time such as:

- I have extra time to do fun things.

- Being awake now means I will sleep even better tomorrow night.

- This is making me realise that I'm concerned about XYZ and I can now put steps in place to fix this problem.

- I get to watch the stars and the night animals and things that everyone else is missing.

- If I really had to be asleep right now, I would be, so I know there is something I am supposed to be learning at this time.

Just because you are not asleep at the time you would like to be, doesn't mean that this is a bad thing. Any negative judgement of the situation causes you to tense up your body, agitate your mind and it leaves you in a state where sleep is very unlikely to occur. When you find yourself awake, use this time to take the following non-stimulating and yet important actions that will increase your success in life and send you back to sleep quickly:

- New Dream.

- Think of all the things you are really grateful for in life.

- Get some of the mundane tasks such as ironing, sock-matching and making packed lunches out of the way so that you'll have more time for other things in the morning.

- Gaze at your treasure map.

- Look at an atlas and think of the places you can visit, especially those with hot sandy beaches and gentle waterfalls.

- Give yourself a facial or smooth on some body moisturiser.

- Listen to a slow piece of classical music.

Another great thing to do before you fall asleep, and any time you wake up during the night, is to send in some powerful and practical mantras or affirmations to your unconscious mind. Here are some that you can start with as you begin to develop some that work best for you:

- I am divinely guided in everything I do.

- I welcome the wealth that the universe sends me now.

- I thank myself for everything I feel, do, and say that adds to my success.

- I enjoy creating success in my life.

- I love myself.

- I am achieving all I have wished for with ease and elegance.

- I enjoy feeling rested and refreshed.

OVER TO YOU

Write up ten affirmations that feel really great to you, ensuring they are in the present tense and stated positively. So, rather than "I will stop gaining weight", say, "I am having fun finding ways to eat healthily and move my body more." Write these up on a sheet of paper and put it in a place where you will say them peacefully during awake-at-night times.

Other things that can disrupt sleep, such as sleep apnoea, are caused by being overweight, so focus on the health parts of this book (Chapter 10) and check in with your doctor. Similarly, many other conditions such as restless legs are solved when great eating and exercise patterns are kept to. So, in a nutshell, if you eat good food, drink water and chill out, you will sleep better and so be ready for the day ahead and for all the magic you are about to make. Sleeping starts in your head, not in the bed.

NINE

YOUR PERSONAL ENVIRONMENT

*"Your outlook upon life, your estimate of yourself,
your estimate of your value are largely coloured by
your environment. Your whole career will be
modified, shaped, moulded by your surroundings."* –
ORISON SWETT MARDEN

For years I found it easier to sleep in hotels than in my own bedroom and it took me ages to figure out that it had a lot to do with the fact that the hotel bedrooms were uncluttered, beautiful and well-aired. Just as we can work more productively in a well-ordered great-looking office, successful sleeping is more easily attainable in a well-planned bedroom. There are dozens of practical steps you can take to vastly improve your sleep environment.

Which of the following best describes your current sleep space?

- A relic that captures the early 1980s so well that a Duran Duran poster would not look out of place.

- A mismatch of every piece of furniture that we couldn't find room for elsewhere in the house.

- The type of place that would make a makeover expert cry in horror and defeat.

141

- More of an office than a bedroom.

- More of a dining room than a bedroom.

- Well, the cats seem to like it.

- Delightful but dull.

- I know there's a bedroom in there somewhere beneath the dirty laundry, and the months-old newspapers and magazines.

What type of bedroom do you aspire to?

- The Lincoln Bedroom in The White House.

- Anything a TV makeover team would do.

- A Scandinavian pale-wood sanctuary of tranquility.

- An eastern lair of gold, silks and exotic prints.

- Something that wouldn't look out of place at a Four Seasons Hotel.

- A place where comfort is king.

- The type of bedroom you would imagine James Bond, Maya Angelou, Tom Cruise, The Queen of England, Madonna, Ralph Lauren or Celine Dion might have.

This is an important area to consider because a better sleep-space is the fastest, most enjoyable way for you to become a more successful sleeper. These steps are for the most part easy, instant and cheap.

Sights

The first phase is to make sure that your room is clutter-free. We're not talking about becoming feng shui masters here, more just getting that pile of magazines into the recycling bin, clothes into wardrobes or laundry baskets, books into order or into the attic. You know, basic Mary Poppins stuff. Why is this so important? Well, the disorder stimulates the conscious mind in an undirected way. Simply ask yourself what feels better, a tidy ordered bedroom or a messy cluttered one? The neater the room, the calmer the mind. It's like having a clear counter when you start cooking.

If it seems that the laundry mountain is too high to ever climb, just tell yourself that you'll pick up twenty items every night before you go to bed or even ten before you go to bed and ten when you wake up. Many people, myself included, missed out on that gene for natural neatness. If the job seems too overwhelming, with boxes of papers and keepsakes amassed over years or decades, get someone else – a friend or professional – to come in and help you. Having control over your physical environment is vital for your psychological well-being. Go on, call someone right now.

Pay particular attention to the colours in your bedroom as these subtly and comprehensively affect your mood and the sensations you feel while in the room. If you tend to wake up feeling hot during the night you might favour cooler tones such as light blues or if you tend to feel too cold, warmer tones such as apricot or terracotta might suit you better. Avoid harsh colours as these will demand too much of your eye and brain.

The teenage tendency for having dozens of posters, photographs and mementos on display is fantastic in so far as it's an expression of who they/you are. If possible, accommodate this trend by having the images displayed on cork boards that can be reversed or covered over when it's time to go to bed. This is the same if you study, work or have loads of self-help materials displayed in your bedroom.

What is the lighting like? The ideal type of lighting isn't too garish and yet is bright enough that you can comfortably get ready for bed.

Is there something in the room that doesn't have good memories associated with it, a chair that reminds you of a love affair gone sour or a plant that reminds you of a horror movie? Get that item out of there! You deserve to be surrounded by things that make you feel incredible.

OVER TO YOU

Take a notebook and pen and sit on your bed in the place you normally sleep. Ask yourself this question: "Ideally, how would I like this room to be?" Without censoring yourself, without listening to those little voices of dissent, without thinking of cost, start to takes notes and make sketches. How many of your ideas can be put into action immediately? Is it possible to paint the walls, move the bed, add a fancy throw and a plant?

Is there something that seems too far beyond your current means, too way-out-there? If so, find a way to compromise until your ideal bedroom arrives into your life. For example, if you would like a magnificent oil painting above the bed, maybe you could borrow a framed print from a friend. If you would like a four-poster bed, perhaps hanging some chiffon to create a canopy might create a similar feeling.

Bring out one or two objects that you associate with good times. A woman I know keeps an undecorated Christmas tree in her room all year round. I like to wake up to the sight of a couple of paintings that I bought on foreign travels. Again, be careful not to make it over-stimulating.

Have fun with this. When your bedroom feels great, when it is both restful and interesting, you will be in a much better physical, mental and spiritual state for the success work of repair, creation and communication that occurs during the night.

Sounds

Now that the room is looking great, ask yourself what you hear during your sleeping hours (that is, what you would hear if you were awake, as well as the sounds that are intrusive enough to wake you and those that won't wake you but will make their way into your unconscious as you sleep). List these sounds on a piece of paper.

We often become immune to the background sounds around us and it's important to remember that we are collecting these sounds in the storehouse. Can you double-glaze a window to cut out the noise of traffic or loud neighbours? Would a letter to your local authority stop the road works happening on your street before dawn? Can the dogs be made comfortable in the kitchen rather than left to roam free along the landing?

What about the sounds made by you and your family? Putting down mats on hardwood floors can soften those footsteps, and deciding to speak to each other in quiet soft voices rather than yelling up and down the hallways also goes a long way to improving the sound environment. If you have one family member who's a night owl, perhaps some agreements as to TV volume and flushing toilets might be arrived at. Snoring family members might like to try nasal strips and other treatments.

Now that you have curtailed the less attractive sounds in your nightscape, it's time to ask how you can add more nurturing and creative sounds.

Would you like to introduce a recording from nature for when you are falling asleep and waking up? These days you can get alarm clocks that gradually wake you with the sound of birdsong or waves crashing on a beach. Even better is to have real nature sounds. Birds can be encouraged by seeds left on a windowsill and ivy can sound great rustling outside. Wind chimes are best when they are subtly chiming in the distance rather than clanging right beside your ear or bashing against the windowpane in a high wind.

Music can be very restful, but avoid anything with lyrics or with too fast or strong a beat. As we now know, the words to a song will go into your unconscious mind when you listen to it at bedtime, so if you do want to listen to songs ensure they have strong positive messages. A good test is to ask yourself whether you would whisper those words into a young child's ear as they fall asleep.

Many people like to listen to motivational CDs as they fall asleep but as the good ones of these can leave you totally revved up and ready to take on the world, they are perhaps best used in the morning. Listening to self-help material during sleep is also not a great idea as it interferes with your natural processing, creating and releasing.

Ask yourself this: What is your favourite soothing sound in the whole world? Kids laughing, leaves rustling, Neil Diamond singing, a gurgling brook, a train whistle, waves on the shore, a carousel, your lover sighing, horses' hooves on a cobbled street, a kitten purring, an engine purring, your father wishing you goodnight, a dog panting, a flute playing in the distance? How can you get that sound into your bedroom by tonight?

Smells

The sense of smell is more closely linked to our memories and emotions than any of the other senses, and yet we can quickly become immune to the smells around us, believing them to be "neutral" whereas, in fact, they hold powerful associations. Did you ever walk into someone's home or sit in their car and wonder how they could live with that ungodly pong? Well, that person just doesn't smell it the way you do. Even though we don't consciously register a smell, its associations affect our mood.

A scent is an "anchor", a way of linking us to an emotion. Think of how you feel when you smell cinnamon, freshly cut grass, a perfume someone wore when you were little, the smell of a photocopier, the same cologne that an ex-partner wore, a cigar, the type of food that once made you ill . . . each of these has the power to bring you back to the feeling you had when you would usually smell it or the feeling you had at an intense moment when you could smell it.

- Just changing the smells in a room can revolutionise how we feel in that space.

- First of all, make sure there are no stuffy or nasty smells going on. Even in the middle of a cold winter, open the windows wide for a few minutes each day (a window slightly open all night is preferable so that fresh air is circulating). Air purifiers with iodising functions are really useful if you're not a big fan of the fresh air.

- It's wise to find an alternative venue for snacking and eating meals as the smells from food can linger, especially of you don't clear away the dishes immediately. (Of course, breakfast-in-bed and other treats are an exception!)

- Train your pets to stay off the bed or preferably out of the bedroom unless you have spent your lifetime becoming completely conditioned to having them there. You can buy simple sonic radar devices to deter animals from straying into and onto certain areas without harming them.

- Smoking in the bedroom, or indeed anywhere, is only undoing all your other great work. Get help for that habit and be smoke-free by this time tomorrow. In a couple of weeks you won't believe the difference. The hundreds of toxic chemicals in a single cigarette are really harmful to your sleep environment as well as to your health and the health of your loved ones. Did you ever see a modern-day hero with a cigarette in their hand? If you are serious about your success, you need to step up and deal with this habit today. What would be the point of being the most successful smoker in the lung-cancer unit of your local hospital? (Okay, so auntie Dot was a smoker and lived to the age of 101 but she'd had a hacking cough since the age of twenty, you could lose small household objects inside her facial wrinkles, she stank to high heaven and in terms of longevity among smokers was the exception rather than the norm! So get over it: smoking sucks at every level.)

- Perfume sprays, incense, aromatic oils and scented candles are all popular ways of creating wonderful aromas to sleep to. Remember to be really careful with candles in the bedroom and extinguish them before you get into bed, in case you get sleepy and drop off sooner than expected. Many house-fires these days are caused by unintentionally abandoned candles.

- How do you personally smell as you get into bed? Most people shower in the morning but thirty seconds spent quickly showering off the sweat of the past few hours and replacing it with the smell of a good gel or soap can evoke more restful feelings. The smells you pick up during the day act as anchors to the events of the day, so the quickest way to shake off your concerns is to take a quick shower and even more restful is a long soak in the bathtub. And there's nothing to stop you putting on perfume or cologne before getting into bed, even years after you consider your partner to be well and truly seduced!

• The air can be made dry and stale with air-conditioning and central heating. Simple solutions are to have a humidifier or a bowl of water with scented oils, which can be made decorative with a couple of flower heads floating in it.

We can often become so immune to the smells around us that we think there's nothing wrong with our bedroom fragrances. Ask a friend to come and sniff out your sleep space and to give a candid opinion. If they turn green before speaking, you've already got your answer!

Safety

Even the soundest of sleepers will wake when there is a sudden noise in the house such as a crashing sound in the kitchen or a loud thud from the living room. Most of the time this will be the sound of a cup slipping off the draining board or a window blowing open but for those first few seconds we invariably imagine it to be Freddy Krueger or some strange person breaking in to steal from us. Unfortunately, this worst-case scenario can come true (a burglar, not Freddy!), so whether it is for peace-of-mind when the cat knocks against a vase or as defence in the face of an intruder, home security is of vital importance. There are experts who specialise in the types of locks and alarms that will best suit your home but do your research and find a company that conducts extensive background checks on its employees. The local police will often provide security advice for free. In the meantime, the following procedures go a long way towards ensuring that you can sleep knowing that your home and the people in it are completely safe.

- Lock all doors, windows, gates, fences and garage doors.

- Replace broken screens, locks and window panes.

- Fit alarms, deadbolts and motion-detector lights.

- Fit timer-switches to make lights downstairs and on the landings go on and off at different times.

- Treat windows with shatter guard.

- Never leave a key under a stone or mat in case of emergencies, always carry keys with you and leave a spare with a neighbour whom you can completely trust.

- Remove from the yard all ladders, trash cans, patio furniture or any other large objects that might help someone gain access to your home.

- If you live alone, give the impression that you don't; add a dog bowl, some clothes or boots from a member of the opposite sex and anything else that might confuse someone watching your house.

Comfort

Considering you spend a third of your life in bed, isn't it worth shelling out a bit of extra cash on your mattress? After all, you wouldn't spend your working day sitting on a wooden crate when you could be in a plush, padded-leather rotating chair so why scrimp on yourself during the hours that are so vital to your success? Night-time discomfort is often the result of a bed that is too hard, too soft, too old, too small or too lumpy for the owner.

Bed linen is also an area where you can easily affect your comfort at night. Pay a visit to the top department store in your town and feel as many different types of sheets as you can. Without looking at any of the prices, decide which feels best to you. Now buy those sheets and use them. This way not only will you feel more comfortable but you will be sending yourself the message that you are worth the very best and this is a wonderful message to be receiving just before you fall asleep and first thing when you wake up. Sheets are best laundered at least once a week to keep them feeling and smelling fresh.

In order to be able to breathe comfortably, keep your bedroom free of dust mites and other allergens by dusting and vacuuming frequently and washing or replacing old pillows, quilts and carpets.

"Dress for Success", the saying goes, and it's no different here. Wearing nightclothes, wearing underwear or going naked are very personal choices. Many people just wear the same type of thing to bed year-in, year-out. Experimenting with cottons, silks, PJs, lingerie, underwear, nightshirts and nudity is the best way of finding out what works best for you. Perhaps cotton pyjamas make you feel restricted and bunch up when you turn in your sleep or perhaps they make you feel cosy and let your skin breathe; it's entirely a matter of what feels great as well as what works for your bed mate. Treating yourself to new nightclothes creates the most wonderful feelings and helps you to relax and sleep better.

OVER TO YOU

Decide what type of nightwear your hero would wear. This might be a top financial trader in silk monogrammed pyjamas, a film actress in pink babydolls, a peace campaigner wearing a non-GMO cotton nightshirt or a fun-loving family man or woman wearing nightclothes with a huge cartoon character that makes the kids smile in the morning. Now find or buy that night-time outfit and you get to sleep and wake up as that person you so admire.

Ask yourself the question, "Who would wear the type of nightclothes you've been sleeping in up until now?"

Old Habits Die Easy

Many people have developed bedtime habits that serve them well in the sense that the habit is fun and feels good but unfortunately it also does them a disservice in that it stops them from getting the kind of sleep that allows the body and the unconscious mind to do their vital work. These habits include late-night eating, watching TV in bed, taking a nightcap and a myriad of other customs.

Man's new best friend is no friend at all as TV drains your energy and replaces it with negative messages. It's an unfortunate development the way many people have televisions and DVDs in their bedrooms these days. Granted, it's fun to be able to relax comfortably in bed and watch a favourite show or a movie as you drift off to sleep. However, when the television stays on during your sleep you have absolutely no control over what is being fed into your unconscious mind. Instead of the mind creating solutions for your successes of the following day and sending out clues for New Dreaming, it is being hypnotised into buying that great set of steak knives. As discussed earlier, watching something that is violent, depressing or pessimistic has a huge effect on how you interact with the world. Having negative scenes fed in during the highly suggestible state which you are in as you fall asleep is even more dangerous. As if that were not damaging enough, it can take longer to fall asleep with the TV on as our brain is stimulated and prevented from winding down after a hectic day. If you feel you need to watch television in order to change focus, do so in another room before moving to your bedroom at a pre-arranged time to start your bedtime routine.

For some people the telephone can be equally intrusive. Make some guidelines for yourself about the type of calls you are prepared to make and receive and the times that you will use the phone. This way you can better judge whether a phone in the bedroom is necessary or advisable.

FUN CHALLENGE

Here's an interesting idea – remove the TV from your bedroom or cover it up and bury the remote for one week. Many people claim that they can only fall asleep in front of the TV but this is simply because they have conditioned themselves to do so and they can just as easily uncondition themselves within a week. See the advice in Chapter 11 on building an empowering bedtime routine.

Another common habit worldwide is using some kind of mind-altering substance at bedtime. The idea of a nightcap – a small alcoholic drink before bedtime – is thankfully going out of fashion. It may induce a similar feeling to the natural drowsiness that comes over you before you drift off but the reality is that it impairs your sleep. The body has to work very hard at processing the sugar and the alcohol and this energy is made unavailable for basic day-to-day (or night-to-night) repair. You also get out of the habit of allowing your natural systems to function as they were designed to in order to get you to sleep, so soon you find yourself dependent on the nightly foe. The same is true for having a spliff, a prescription medication, an over-the-counter cough or cold medicine that induces drowsiness, a cigarette or cigar or anything else that messes with the body and brain chemistry.

Make a decision now that you are in control of your life, including the type of sleep you get.

On the first day that you decide that you will fall asleep naturally (would now be a good time?), wear yourself out during the afternoon and early evening with a long walk or other physical activity. Take your time to wind down physically and mentally that evening and set yourself a bedtime routine that you will follow for the next two weeks as you recondition yourself to be a more successful sleeper. Ways to help you wind down naturally include a warm bath, a massage from someone or lying on a self-massage mat, sipping chamomile tea or listening to a meditation or relaxation recording.

After the first week write up notes on the benefits you feel on throwing out this old habit and re-read those notes if ever you feel tempted to slip back. It is easy to reset an old pattern even by rerunning it on one occasion, so telling yourself that you'll watch bedroom TV or take the pill or the glassful "just this once" is really just fooling yourself and undoing all your great work.

If you have had a habit for over forty years, find a way to reduce the bad side-effects; perhaps have a smaller drink along with a glass of water or have a timer that switches off your TV after half an hour.

What else can you change about your habits and environment that will empower your sleep time?

TEN

YOUR HEALTH

"Take care of your body with steadfast fidelity. The soul must see through these eyes alone, and if they are dim, the whole world is clouded." – GOETHE

It's the body that sleeps and so it's only common sense that the better shape the body is in the better the sleep will be. Then when you sleep better it benefits the body even further in an upward spiral.

Taking responsibility for your body is something people tend to think of only when a trip to the beach is looming or when the body becomes toxic and cannot fight off infection which is manifested as illness. Needless to say, in order to be successful in any area of life, energy and vigour are paramount.

Food

What, how and when you eat plays a vital role ensuring you sleep powerfully and in guaranteeing that your body is working at its optimum.

OVER TO YOU

The first step is to take an honest assessment as people easily delude themselves about just how many "treats" and "exceptions" are going on. What did you eat today and yesterday, and when did you eat these things? List the meals and the times here.

_____

_____

_____

How did you feel at each meal; relaxed, rushed, excited, stressed, enraptured, bored, disassociated (aka "nothing"), giddy, powerful, loving, anxious . . . ? How did what you ate and when you ate it help or hinder your sleep in its job of repairing the body?

The body is the machine that takes all the action to make your dreams come true – it lifts the phone, it generates the ideas, it hugs people, it walks from the car to the office, it speaks and laughs, it dances and reaches, writes and mixes. It is the "doer", the link between the desire and the result. So it is absolutely imperative that your wonderful, valuable body is in great shape for this amazing project.

You can make your sleep-time infinitely more effective by choosing some simple changes to what you put in your mouth.

Many people give their body an almost impossible task to accomplish during the sleeping hours. They eat sugary, unhealthful foods that the body then has to expend great effort to digest and to get rid of the toxins (poisons) that are building up. Eating empty calories rather than nutritious foods means that very little real energy is available for the repair work which the body is supposed to do while we sleep.

There is so much debate these days about what are good foods and what are not good foods. The simple answer is that non-processed foods contain less sugar and less harmful fats and chemical additives than processed foods. The best way to take in the vitamins, minerals and thousands of micro-nutrients needed to feel great and do great things is to eat what are termed "living" or "live" foods. Live foods are basically anything that grows from the ground and has not had its enzymes destroyed by cooking. So wheat is a live food and bread is not, tomatoes are a live food but pizza is not, a potato is a live food but French fries are not. Eggs, meat and cheese are not live foods, but the body can process them in very small amounts. However, if you really want to know how it feels to be healthy, try replacing any meat and dairy with no meat and non-dairy alternatives for a couple of weeks.

Healthy eating begins at the healthy shopping stage (or the healthy ordering stage if you are a restaurant fanatic). Just put loads of the following foods into your shopping cart, clear out any non-live foods from your kitchen and eventually you'll work out a way to make them taste really good to you.

- Aubergines, courgettes, tomatoes, yellow/red/orange bell peppers, leeks, onions, carrots, broccoli, cabbage, mangetout, sugar-snap peas, garden peas, asparagus, artichokes, celery, lettuce leaves, and any other favourite vegetable.

- Lentils, split peas, sweet peas, mung beans, red beans, flageolet beans, haricot beans, black-eyed peas, chick peas.

- Sweet potato, potato (in moderation), butternut squash, pumpkin, yams, sweet corn, parsnips.

- Hazelnuts, cashew nuts, walnuts, pine nuts, almonds, sunflower seeds, pumpkin seeds.

- Oats, barley, wheat, couscous, quinoa, wild rice.

- Any type of fruit (must be eaten separately from other foods and only once or twice a day). Sugary fruits such as bananas, strawberries and mango are best avoided. Great fruits include blueberries, raspberries and papaya.

- Extra virgin olive oil, walnut oil, Udo's choice oil.

Log on to www.SleepingYourWayToSuccess.com for some healthy recipes to get you started. You can prepare these any way you like, as long as you add any oils *after* cooking and cook for as short a time as possible. Boiling doesn't work so well as the nutrients go into the water and the good stuff in them is drained away. Roasting or frying in a wok with a liquid other than oil works best. There are some great vegan cookbooks and if you eat meat and dairy you can add bits of these too, ensuring that every meal is at least seventy per cent vegetable-based and the meat is organically and locally sourced.

While you're at it, get over the idea that breakfast must be processed juice, cereal and breads. Breakfasts that keep you feeling great are those that have fruit and vegetables as their base. If salad for breakfast seems strange, have it in a wholemeal soft tortilla wrap as you get used to this new way of eating. Who says pancakes feel or taste better than a vegetable and tofu scramble? If you think they do, this is a sign that you have a sugar addiction. A couple of weeks without any sugar will re-set your taste buds and your entire digestive system as well as clearing out all the nasty stuff from your blood. And, on that note, here's the way you can rapidly accelerate your success as you step a little outside your comfort zone – try a new way of eating for ten days. Come on, it's only ten days and at worst you'll have eaten better for over a week; at best you'll start to introduce better foods into your and your family's lives, transforming your energy and the way you feel.

Note: if you have trouble sleeping and you choose to keep eating processed and/or sugary foods like pastas and breads, then you are entirely responsible for your sleep challenges. You can no longer refer to it as "insomnia" and claim to be unlucky. My apologies if this sounds harsh, but it's the simple truth; you get a result based on your action. The same thing goes for caffeine, which you'll be reading a lot about very soon.

When eating at a restaurant or café, you can usually put together a nice healthy meal by asking for all the vegetable side orders to be served to you on one plate or by finding the meal with the most vegetables and other live foods. These days many restaurants are preparing healthy and delicious alternatives as part of their standard menus.

When you stick to a mostly live food way of eating every day, you not only sleep, look and feel better, you also lose any extra weight you've been carrying.

Eating within two hours of going to sleep is not advisable, simply because during the night you want the body to repair and rest and not be spending its energy digesting your last meal. If you are so hungry that the pangs are stopping you from getting to sleep, then eat a small handful of something non-sugary. A cup of warm soya milk or soup is best, some vegetable paté, leftover veggies or salad. A spoonful of peanut butter is good too, because it contains tryptophan, an amino acid that tends to increase sleepiness. (Make sure you go for a non-sugared kind.) Avoid fruit as these are too high in natural sugars to be helpful. I find that planning a really exciting breakfast prevents me from snacking late at night, as much of the eating we do is prompted by boredom and habit rather than necessity.

Caffeine is the Enemy of Your Dream Life

Caffeine is the big enemy of sleep. There are so many false personal beliefs attached to this drug and so much money spent pushing it as a natural lifestyle choice that it's no wonder so many people are exhausted during the day. A typical caffeinated day might involve several cups of tea or coffee, cola-type sodas with meals and all-day snacks from candy bars to "health bars" laced with chocolate. The drug companies then have the nerve to invent conditions called "Daily Fatigue Syndrome" or "Excessive Daytime Sleepiness", and claim to be able to cure them! Everything you need to do in order to feel rested is already available to you, just as everything you need to have a fitful night's sleep and wake up exhausted is also available to you. You get to choose.

I am going to really talk about caffeine in depth, as most people who claim to be insomniacs or who claim to be tired during the day indulge in this legalised drug. I am happy to risk sounding fanatical, but then so did people in the 1950s who talked about damage and death from cigarettes. Caffeine is the major method that people use to kill their chance of sleeping in a way

165

that makes them fully energised for creating and building their amazing lives. Caffeine kills your dreams.

Some people have become not only addicted to caffeine but to the rituals surrounding it, to the extent that they believe their lives would be far less without the drug.

Ask yourself this, "When you visualise yourself being successful, are you grabbing a coffee on your way into your impressive job or sipping a cappuccino in a sidewalk cafe in Europe?" If so, change the picture so your personal assistant is handing you some freshly squeezed juice, or change that cup of foam for a tall cold glass of lime or raspberry cordial or whatever feels great to you.

FACT: Over 90 per cent of adults in the Western world take caffeine every day in the form of coffee, sodas and chocolate.

FICTION: Caffeine makes you alert. I know that you may feel that way, but what you are actually feeling is a false jolt of nervous energy, counteracting your exhaustion in the short term. This leaves your body even more tired very soon after and also leaves it more acidic, so that the body is less capable of getting the oxygen through your bloodstream into all the places it needs to be.

The Science Bit

When we think of coffee we often think of warm and friendly coffee shops enticing us with a variety of exciting concoctions. Most times this lovely picture easily wins the battle against the abstract and distant notion that caffeine is bad for you. Getting a clear picture of what caffeine does can go a long way to getting you to feel differently about this harmful drug. No, it probably won't kill you anytime soon, but it will rob you of the energy needed to achieve your ultimate goals quickly and effortlessly.

Caffeine is a crystal powder chemical called trimethylxanthine that manipulates certain channels in the brain.

When you are falling asleep, a chemical called adenosine binds to its receptors and you get drowsy as nerve cell activity is slowed down. This also makes the blood vessels expand, so more oxygen gets in during sleep. Caffeine looks to the body like adenosine, so it binds to the receptor, but it speeds up the nerve-cell energy instead of slowing it down. So then the pituitary gland thinks there's a big emergency going on in the body and it tells the adrenal glands to produce adrenaline. This makes your heart beat faster, your pupils dilate, your muscles tighten and it causes the liver to release sugar into your bloodstream so that you have extra energy to cope with this "emergency". Once the "emergency" is over, the body is in a less good state than it was before taking the drug.

Caffeine also increases your dopamine levels, making you feel good for a while but soon after the initial emergency jolt, you are left with feelings of fatigue, depression and irritability, usually causing you to reach for more caffeine.

Putting yourself into this fake state of emergency means that there is more mending for the body to do during the night and when the body fails to catch up on its mending, we feel tired during the day.

The half-life of caffeine in the body is about six hours. So if you have a big cup of coffee with 200mg of caffeine at six o'clock, there is still 100mgs in your body at midnight. You might be able to fall asleep but it will not be a good, deep sleep.

Getting off Caffeine Easily

You first need to assess how much caffeine you are taking at the moment. Write the answers in beside the questions so that you can't avoid the reality.

- How many cups of coffee did you have yesterday?

- How many cups of coffee have you had so far today?

- What was the strength of the coffee?

- How many cups of tea did you have yesterday?

- How many cups of tea have you had today?

- What was the strength of the tea?

- How much cola-based soda did you have yesterday?

- How much cola-based soda have you had today?

- What was the strength of the soda?

- How much chocolate did you eat yesterday?

- How much chocolate have you eaten in the last week?

- How much chocolate have you eaten today?

- In answering the above, did you hear any little excuses creeping in, such as:

  - *"Well, yesterday was unusual because . . ."?*
  - *"Well, I don't drink as much coffee as I did last month . . ."?*
  - *"At least I don't drink as much tea as Debbie across the hall . . ."?*
  - *"But it was organic . . ."?*
  - *"I really need it because I'm kept awake all night with the baby . . ."?*
  - *Other . . .*

- What have been your beliefs about caffeine in the past?

- What are your current beliefs about caffeine?

- What would be some even better beliefs to have about caffeine?

- If you were to substitute something tasty for the

caffeine products you used to consume, what would those new tasty things be?

If you feel that you need caffeine every day; if this whole section irritates you; if you feel anxious at the idea of not having any caffeine today or tomorrow . . . then you are probably addicted. You can argue against this, but the fact remains.

If you are comparing yourself to the rest of the population in terms of caffeine consumption, that's not helpful, as we're an unhealthy society. Instead, why not compare yourself to the fittest, healthiest person you know, not in order to feel bad and beat yourself up about how far you are behind their standard but in order to get a measure on where you are and what you need to do in order to get to your ideal state of health.

Finding alternatives to caffeine is very important because it is the number one stealer of sleep in the world today and because being caffeine-free puts you on the high road to success, instantly. It's easier to choose not to take caffeine when you have some great alternatives, especially when these are available in the places you like to frequent.

One great coffee substitute is hot oat-milk/rice-milk. When I was first introduced to peppermint, fruit and herb teas, I couldn't stand them. I think it was because I was comparing them to the sugary, milky brown teas that I'd been downing ten times a day since the age of twelve. I'd become a bit of a connoisseur of teas, favouring broken Orange Pekoe, Earl Grey and Darjeeling, so it was hard to think that I'd have to give up this stylish, entertaining and tasty part of my lifestyle. It took me a month of drinking a small cup of chamomile tea every day before I began to actually look forward to the ritual. I still kept my cute teapot with the smiling purple cats and I can still go into a little shop in New York and come out with a tiny brown paper bag of some untried brew, except now it's some exotic fruit or herb infusion in the bag. At night a cup of chamomile tea is great for calming down your mind and body in a natural way.

Decaffeinated coffee is not advised as it keeps you craving the coffee taste which will make you more likely to go back to caffeinated coffee and the goal is to be caffeine-free forever. Like most people, I love the smell of coffee, so I happily sit in a coffee shop smelling the Brazilian and Costa Rican aromas while drinking my hot soya milk.

Alternatives for chocolate are easier as so many sweet treats are available, from flapjacks to toffees to cakes and cookies in vanilla, nut, fruit and other flavours. Remember to keep them to a minimum, as sugar doesn't help in your bid for the top of the world.

When coming off caffeine, you may experience headaches, slight nausea, a cold feeling in your hands or other side effects. This is the body correcting the damage and getting back in line with how it should be working. Isn't it better to get things fixed and then keep them that way, rather than going back onto the caffeine after you have detoxed or just continuing to upset your system with it on an ongoing basis?

OVER TO YOU

Write up on a piece of paper one special goal that you would like to achieve which depends on having real (not fake and inconsistent) energy. Really do this, not just in your head.

Take one action RIGHT NOW that will help you to reduce or eliminate caffeine from your life. This might be:

- Pouring a can of cola down the drain.

- Asking your partner to support you in cutting out caffeine for one week.

- Buying some non-caffeinated (rather than decaffeinated) fruit and herb teas.

- Trying a hot soya milk, honey and cinnamon drink from your local coffee shop or café or making it at home.

Hydrating

We can survive only a few days without water. The body is 70 per cent water and it is necessary to every function performed. Without water, the brain closes down and this starts in a small way before we even get thirsty. Try this: the next time you can't work out a problem or the next time you feel stuck, drink a large glass of water and notice how within a minute the task suddenly becomes effortless. When we are dehydrated (i.e. we don't have enough water inside us) the red blood vessels clump together (much as they do when we eat sugary and other acid-forming foods) and when they clump together they move more slowly around the body and carry less oxygen with them.

Other liquids, such as processed juices, sodas, tea and coffee do not do the same job as water, even though they have a high water content. Regularly sipping from a bottle of water is a vital habit to develop. If your kids (or co-workers) are cranky, rather than giving them sweets or biscuits in an effort at appeasement, try having them drink some water and watch their mood magically and immediately improve.

We often confuse thirst with hunger, as the triggers can feel the same. We can think we are hungry but what we really are craving is the water in the food. So the next time you have a yen for a snack and yet you have recently eaten, drink a pint of water instead and notice how you feel.

A fully hydrated person will sleep much better than a dehydrated person. Having said that, the dreaded trek to the bathroom in the middle of the night (you know, the one where you stub your toe and get blinded by the bathroom light and wake the baby as you trip over a wet towel) is best avoided. If you are hydrating during the day the body will not feel the need to rid itself of toxins (i.e. pee) during the night. This doesn't mean you should drink loads of water before bedtime; instead, drink a pint of water as soon as you wake up and have finished New Dreaming and then sip your way through a tumbler of water every hour until ninety minutes before your bedtime.

Having enough water in your body means that you are not adding any extra stresses to an already maxed-out machine. When you have the right amount of water on board, your body can replenish cells and restore energy as it was designed to do, much of which happens as you sleep.

Move that Body!

Working out too close to bedtime will mean that your body has not had sufficient time to slow down and you may find yourself lying there, alert and ready for action. However, exercise – both cardio (where you pant and sweat a bit) and load-bearing (such as lifting weights or carrying heavy shopping bags) – is vital for ensuring you feel great, stay fit and healthy and are able to sleep well at night. Many people find that a simple thirty-minute walk after dinner cures any sleep challenges they might have been experiencing.

Modern lifestyles are pretty static; we sit behind the

wheel of a car, then sit behind a desk, then behind the wheel again before sitting on a sofa all night. There is a tension that comes about in the body through not moving enough. Simply put, if you don't move your body during the day, your body will be moving at night, as restless muscles cause you to twitch and move about to try and get comfortable. Move more to sleep better.

So many people claim that they do not have the time to exercise and yet they spend over an hour every night lying there awake. Think of all the time you lose through inefficiency due to fatigue or through just slumping. Remember, what we are doing here is making sure that there is a real difference between the waking and sleeping body. The waking body is moving and energised, while the sleeping body is in a deep sleep all night. So many people are "stealing" rest in the form of being inactive at the exact time that the body needs to be creating energy through expending energy. The more you move, the more your body will feel like moving. It is not the case that you can't move your body because you feel tired; it's that you feel tired because your body isn't moving.

Simple ways to kick-start some energy (especially if you are in the habit of being sluggish first thing in the morning) include jumping up and down ten times on a mini-trampoline just outside the bedroom; or dancing like a fool to some song that might be cheesy but always gets your groove on. I admit that I still occasionally have those mornings when I feel that getting up out of bed would be a near-impossible feat requiring the courage of gods, and at these times I stay lying down and just wave my arms around. It probably looks bizarre, but it does get my energy levels revved up enough that I can move to a standing position.

Some people like to don running shoes and pound the pavement first thing on waking, but many find this too big a shock to the system. If this is the case for you, then why not start with some gentle stretching exercises first thing? Young children, even babies from eighteen months, love to join in with this, so you can make it a family ritual. What a great gift to give your kids – the life-habit of making your body strong and flexible instead of the life-habit of watching cartoons.

Another excuse that people use is that a part of their body being injured makes it impossible for them to exercise. Rather than focusing on what you can't do, let's look at what you can do. If you have sore joints, you can swim; if you have a bad leg, you can work your upper body with hand weights; if you are recovering from an illness, you can ask your doctor what exercise you can safely do. Most people who work out daily report that they sleep soundly every night. Also, having less unhealthy body fat reduces the chances of sleep apnoea, a dangerous condition where the person stops breathing for extended periods while asleep. (If you or your partner have this, then you need to tell your primary health care provider immediately.)

While you are asleep, your breathing becomes deeper, as oxygen is vital to the repair work being carried out. The stronger the muscles that support your breathing and the healthier your heart is, the more oxygen will be available for this process. So people who keep their bodies in a state of health and fitness not only find it easier to sleep, they also benefit more from their sleep time. Remember also that the brain is part of the bio-chemical system of the body and so you can't expect for that to be working out your challenges while you sleep if the energy has been diverted to digestion or circulation.

OVER TO YOU

List three ways that you used to love to move when you were a child or a teenager and incorporate one of them back into your life this week. Suggestions:

- Dancing to your favourite band
- Walking to your friend's house
- Cycling to the shops
- Rambling through the fields with your dog
- Ice-skating or rollerblading
- Horseback riding
- Surfing

- Skateboarding
- Skipping
- Bouncing a ball
- Walking up and down the shopping centre all day
- Splashing in puddles
- Basketball
- Chasing butterflies
- Playing Frisbee
- Football
- Swinging on a tyre tied to a tree
- Hurling
- Rowing a boat
- Doing handstands
- Swimming
- Jumping up and down on the sofa.

ELEVEN

RELATIONSHIPS AND LIFESTYLE

"People who say they sleep like a baby usually don't have one." – LEO J BURKE

Your success is built and shared with the people around you, your family, friends, workmates and acquaintances. Working with a great team is all the fun, some of the challenge and an absolutely necessary component when it comes to living an outstanding life. In terms of getting the most out of those magical seven or eight hours of sleep, the person you spend time with before, during and after sleep is your most important partner for success. Hopefully they've been playing along with you as you change your sleep ways to more productive ones, but if not there are still ways that you can take them into consideration and move with them on and up to achieving absolute success.

Intimate Partner
It's an honour and a privilege to get to sleep beside another human being. Your moods and ways subtly

influence each other as you sleep and as you start and finish each day in their company. The most important part of having a bed mate is to be grateful for their presence and to respect them enough to ensure that you yourself are a pleasure to share the sheets with.

Ask your partner what they love about sharing a bed with you and then what it is they feel you could work on together to make it even better. You can then, with their permission, share your thoughts about what is great and what you can both do to increase your pleasure, relaxation and success.

Check yourself against this list to find out if you are a Sleep Mate From Heaven or a Bed Hog From Hell.

- How do you smell getting into bed?

  o I smell of whatever garlic or curry meal I just ate.

  o I smell of the shower gel he/she specially bought for me, knowing it's my favourite.

- How do you look when getting into bed?

  o I wear my oldest, comfiest sweatshirt and shorts.

  o I wear the pyjamas/babydolls my partner likes me in, which feel great but end up thrown to the floor way before we fall asleep!

- What mood are you generally in when you get into bed?

○ I'm pissed off that I didn't get everything done.

○ I'm relaxed and playful and ready for some quality time with my partner as we drift off.

• What is your standard pillow talk?

○ I moan about work and list everything I have to do i in the morning.

○ I tell my bed mate how much they mean to me and ask them how they are feeling.

• How is your bedclothes etiquette?

○ I will do whatever it takes to ensure that the sheets are fully wrapped around me and cannot be prized away.

○ I make sure that both of us are warm, comfortable and happy.

What else can you do to make the bed a pleasant place for you to be as a couple?

Unfortunately, issues from the day or ongoing problems can make the bed a less-than-relaxing place to be. The good news is that there are easy and practical steps we can take to turn these challenges into opportunities for success.

OVER TO YOU

Imagine you had to lie on a small bed right up-close to something that made you feel uncomfortable – a strange dog, a box of needles, a snake, a pile of mud, a bowl of bad food. How would that make you feel? What quality of sleep would you get in this scenario, good or poor?

Now imagine you get to snuggle up beside something absolutely delightful – a clean cashmere sweater, rose petals, a childhood teddy bear – whatever would be lovely to you. How would that sleep differ from the first?

Now, I'd never liken your partner to a dog or a snake, but I do want to highlight how important it is to feel at ease in your own bed. If there are issues from your waking life that have not been dealt with before bedtime, this conflict will be carried deeper into your unconscious as you sleep. (If your problems with your partner involve addiction, abuse or anything that frequently makes you feel unsafe or upset, please get professional help immediately.)

For many couples, the few minutes before they fall asleep is all the time they have to check in with each other and catch up on what has been happening during the day. Sometimes this means discussing uncomfortable topics such as debt, problems with the kids, health or marital troubles or challenges each of you has faced during the day. Instead of allowing this to happen, schedule ten minutes in some other room, maybe sitting on the sofa or at the kitchen table, and say anything awkward or pedestrian that you feel needs to be said *before* you start to get ready for bed.

Many couples will watch a few of hours of television together before switching off and having ten minutes' pillow talk. If this sounds familiar to you, why not turn off the TV an hour before bedtime so you can discuss personal, household and family issues in a more relaxed, more constructive way.

Continue speaking when you get into bed, avoiding any subject that is practical, motivational or that might cause either of you to feel bad. Keep this as a time for telling each other how lucky you are to be with each other, how proud you feel of your partner, how excited you are about going on vacation with them . . . You might also tell fun, light stories from your day. Of course, this is also an ideal time to make love.

The big rule: ONLY SPEAK GOOD IN THE BED!!

If you have a sudden burning need to discuss something negative – for example, if one of you is feeling unloved after sex or feeling rejected because you didn't have sex, if you suddenly remember that you didn't book the flight for that holiday – both of you need to get up and move into another room to have that chat. If your partner is not prepared to do so, then write down the thought in a notebook and take it up with them in the morning (when it will often have magically reduced in size and importance). If they don't have the energy to go into another room then they don't have the energy to listen to you constructively. And that's fine; we can't be "on form" all the time.

OVER TO YOU

Breathing in tandem with your partner for a couple of minutes before you go to bed, taking deep breaths in and out at the same time, has amazing results. It causes you to feel even closer to the other person, it steadies your own body and mind, it imitates the deep breathing of sleep and fools your body into feeling drowsier.

Every shared bedroom has areas of conflict and compromise. For example, with one couple I know, the man can only fall asleep with the windows wide open and if they were living in Siberia this would still be the case. She, on the other hand, finds it hard to fall asleep to the sound of traffic and she really feels the cold, even in rooms that others find warm. So they sleep with the windows part of the way open and she has an extra blanket on her side. If she wakes up feeling cold and he is fast asleep, she will close a window, and if he later wakes up and needs to open it again there is no blame or annoyance. They both want the exact same outcome: for both of them to get the sleep they need. The other stuff is just details and something to laugh about.

Sometimes it may seem that you both have entirely different bedtime needs and you must ensure that these needs are met while guarding the intimacy of your sleep-lives together. If one person needs more sleep, they might often go to bed feeling lonely as they listen to their lover watching TV in another room. In order to remedy this, you can both go to bed at the same time, and then the person who needs fewer hours' bed-rest can get up again once their partner is asleep. If one person wants thirty teddy bears in the bed and the other wants none, compromise with two bears or make sure your partner is having such a good time in bed that they're not even thinking about teddy bears. If one person has to get up early, then they can ensure that their clothes for the next day are ready in the bathroom or a downstairs room and the partner who sleeps later can take all the advice in this book to ensure that they are sleeping soundly and have set their sleep clock, making it easier to stay asleep while their partner gets up. Too many couples opt to sleep in separate rooms and then wonder why they start to "drift apart".

But what if your partner's night-time snoring or restlessness is preventing you from sleeping well? The first step is to approach them as the solution and not as the problem. That means asking for their help rather than accusing them of spoiling your night, phrasing it in ways such as, "Darling, I have a problem sleeping; you see I'm such a light sleeper that when you move I find myself waking up. I'd love to hear any ideas you might have for me." They might then say that they find it hard to sleep right through the night and you can start a discussion on how to help that. Express concern for their health and well-being rather than complaining that your own sleep is being compromised, while remembering that their health is their responsibility and your health is yours. Equally, marching them off to the doctor's office will make them feel controlled and disapproved of and cause them to be resistant to any snoring solutions.

I once had a boyfriend who, if he was really tired or feeling under the weather, could sometimes wake me with his snoring. I decided from the very start that I would never feel annoyed by this and instead would take it as a reminder to be grateful for having this lovely man asleep beside me. During the relationship we had so many nights sleeping thousands of miles apart that being awake and watching him sleep was a huge blessing. I would sometimes take the opportunity to whisper very quietly into his ear, saying, "I'm so proud of you, you are so wonderful, you are so relaxed and happy." Sometimes just tapping him on the shoulder would cause him to move into a position where the snoring stopped. The fact that I wasn't all wound-up about it made it easier for me to drift back to sleep. So Anthony Burgess wasn't necessarily right when he said, "Laugh and the world laughs with you; snore and you sleep alone."

Kids

I often hear people who are raising children listing all the things they can't do because of the extra demands on their time, energy and focus. They say that having children makes it impossible to get a good night's sleep or to be able to have an organised bedtime or morning time. And yet there are other parents who say that having children is the very reason why they insist on having great sleep habits. So to those parents who claim that little ones hamper their sleeping, I always ask the question, "Okay, so what *can* you do?" What things that you've learned from this book can you make happen? What can you adapt? What can you include your kids in? Can you make their sleep environment more relaxing and healthier?

What beliefs about sleep have you passed on to your kids, either knowingly or accidentally through your own sleep behaviours?

When you write up on a piece of paper exactly what you do with the kids in terms of getting them to bed, getting yourselves to bed and getting everyone up in the morning, you can start to get clarity on why certain aspects work well and other aspects don't work. You might see that you are putting kids to bed an hour after they have eaten dessert and so they are buzzing with sugar. No wonder they don't go to bed easily. Or perhaps they know that bedtime is a movable feast and so pull out every trick in the book, knowing there is

187

always a chance that they might be able to push for an extra thirty minutes. Is it that you are waking yourselves and them just in time to rush the getting-ready processes, promising nothing but stress on waking, causing everyone in the family to try to squeeze more time from the day's end – them with toys, you with surfing the Internet? Are bedtime and wake-up time a battle which you only sometimes win?

Exactly how to motivate your children is a huge topic, beyond the scope of this book, but there are many great books on child psychology which will be really useful to you in designing how you want your kids' and your own sleep time to be. Yes, it does take more time and care, but having kids needn't mean any less sleep once they are beyond the tiny baby stage.

If you do have a case of a sick child or one who occasionally wants you in the middle of the night, you need to be clear on what your job is. Try to wake up at your usual time the next morning and, if possible, return yourself and your child to your own beds so that who sleeps where is clear and consistent.

Some people are fans of co-sleeping with babies and if this is your personal choice, please ensure that you have a plan for when the baby or child will move into their own space. You will also need a contingency for when and where you and your partner get to connect sexually so that this key component of your relationship is kept healthy, alive and passionate.

It really isn't a case of having-of-kids = lack-of-sleep; it's a case of lack-of-planning = lack-of-sleep. Many parents will go to bed at midnight, knowing that one or both of them will be woken at six o'clock. If this is the case, take charge and get yourself into bed by ten. Others will make up sleep arrangements on the hoof, adopting an "anything for a quiet life" strategy: if the toddler screams loud enough, they get to come into Mummy and Daddy's bed; if the teen mouths off enough, they get given the so-called compromise of "another hour but then it really is lights off". Parents often have strong beliefs about what constitutes good parenting: either leaving a baby to cry or picking them up immediately; allowing toddlers to sleep with a soother or weaning them off dummies at a young age; letting a teen choose their own bedtime or having a strict lights-out for all siblings simultaneously. Whatever your beliefs, you must have routines to back these up and the routines must be consistent and clearly understood by all involved with both parents agreeing on the family sleep plan.

OVER TO YOU

Write out what the sleep times and habits are of everyone in your family. Then write out the reasons for these habits, such as:

- Wendy (mother) goes to sleep at ten because she is usually tired after watching the reality show on TV at nine o'clock.

- Tony (father) goes to bed at eleven because he likes an hour to himself to check his e-mails and the day's stock market reports.

- Natasha (five-year-old) wakes up at three o'clock because she knows her Dad will get her a glass of water, talk to and cuddle her for fifteen minutes and carry her back to bed.

- Chris (one-year-old) wakes up at six, as this is his natural sleep cycle, having been put to bed at seven in the evening.

Can you see ways in which the family above might improve their family sleep patterns? Perhaps walking Natasha straight back to bed with no talking when she wakes up or putting the baby to bed an hour later or Tony checking his e-mail at the same time that Wendy watches her TV show?

How can your family get their bedtime schedules and habits into sync?

At a certain age (and you get to determine this age) children really need to be in their own beds at night in order for each family member to have the physical space they need to sleep without getting knocked in the head by someone's elbow or woken by adult snoring. If you do like having your kids in the bed, create a ritual such as them joining you there on Sunday morning, but make sure that random drop-ins and night-time visits are not allowed. It can be tempting when you are half-asleep to let them stay, but if you get them back to their own beds every time without exception, they will soon get the message. Creating exceptions to the rules due to illness, tiredness or for whatever reason only creates doubt and weakens the child's certainty about what is and is not allowed. Children thrive on boundaries so ensure that you set firm and fair ones around bedtime, beds and other sleep issues.

Routine

What you do during the hour before you go to bed is what most strongly influences the type of sleep you have that night.

What does your last hour before bed look like? Perhaps like one of the following:

- On the phone for the first thirty minutes, ten minutes grabbing a sandwich, fifteen minutes putting the final details to tomorrow's presentation, five minutes showering and getting into bed.

- Ten minutes brushing teeth and changing into nightclothes, ten minutes talking to spouse, forty minutes reading a book you heard about through your local book club.

- Whole hour spent watching some old movie or

flicking between stations, eating pizza and drinking beer before falling asleep *in situ* as the TV drones on.

- Thirty minutes getting the kids' clothes ready for the next day, ten minutes changing and brushing teeth, ten minutes complaining about how tired you are, ten minutes digging something semi-clean from the laundry basket for you to wear in the morning.

Did any of these strike a chord? What might be a better bedtime scenario?

Having the same routine every night will actually train your brain that it is now time for sleep. It's the same principle as reading the same bedtime story to a child and putting them to bed at the same time every night. Set yourself a bedtime and aim to be free to begin your routine at least an hour ahead of that bedtime.

Here are some alternative pick-and-mix suggestions for your twilight hour:

- Ten minutes getting your own clothes and work materials ready so you can take your time in the morning.

- Ten minutes making your bedroom look, sound, smell and feel lovely.

- Twenty minutes soaking in a relaxing lavender oil bath.

- Fifteen minutes writing in a journal all the things you are grateful for and proud of from that day.

- Ten minutes visualising your ideal life in clear detail.

- Fifteen minutes telling your lover all the things you have enjoyed doing with them that day.

- Ten minutes playing the guitar.

You can of course double up on some, things such as visualising while in the bath or serenading your lover with guitar tunes.

OVER TO YOU

Using some of the ideas above, design your own bedtime routine.

What else would feel good to you as a bedtime routine? Time with your partner? Time with your dog or cat? Prayer? Chatting calmly on the phone with someone? Reading something? Listening to music? Watering the houseplants?

Carry out that routine tonight and notice how it made you feel. Wonderful? Guilty? Frustrated? What needs to change in order that you can feel great with a bedtime routine that really serves you and those around you? What new beliefs might be useful?

Perhaps there are other aspects to your life that result in your needing to be even more vigilant about how you plan your sleep.

Do you care for someone, an elderly or sick person who needs you throughout the night? Ask yourself if there is some way that through family or through the authorities, this responsibility might be shared, allowing you to get to sleep through the night at least a couple of times per week.

If you do shift work, then having black-out curtains and perhaps a light-box to simulate the natural triggers for sleep will enable you to mimic the sleep cycle of those who sleep more conventional hours. The same thing goes for those who travel long distances across time zones. Ask yourself if there is some way that you can normalise your sleeping patterns, perhaps by working in a different way.

Do you suffer from some illness or disability that makes it a challenge to sleep for more than a couple of hours at a time? You will find that the suggestions in this book will go a long way towards helping with this, and a chat with your doctor about how you have been sleeping and how you would prefer to sleep will mean that they can help you to achieve this. Many people presume that lack of sleep must be suffered through and fail to tell health-care providers what is going on. Sleeping powerfully will go a long way to getting you feeling healthy and fit once again.

For many, it's a simple case of stress winning out over sleep, as many people find themselves doing the midnight-mind-marathon.

One common experience is that of living through a challenging day and then having all the details of that day, all the anxieties, all the possible solutions and all the ways it could get worse running around your brain as soon as you hit the sack. Running over the details of the waking hours is guaranteed to make your brain think that it is still time for being alert. If you are still combing through scenarios in your head at bedtime, then go and sit in another room and write down all the things that are concerning you and all the actions that you intend to take the next day in order to make the situation better. Once you have these written down, you can safely let them go free from your head, as they are all contained on the page. Next, before you go into the bedroom, decide what would be the downside to letting your head race all night, and what would be the upside to getting a good night's sleep.

Once you get into bed, put something else firmly into your head so that the nagging thoughts have no room to appear on your inner stage. Imagine a circus or a beach or somewhere that you need to concentrate to paint a full picture and yet it is a fun, restful picture you are painting. Make things happen in that picture – does the clown throw coloured confetti over the crowd or does a windsurfer sail past? In this case, it's best not to paint future pictures from your own life as you would be highly likely to slip back into thinking about whatever was troubling you earlier. Soft music can give your mind something to cling to once the details of the day have been banished. Often we mull over "stuff" because we want to be successful in our endeavours, so it's important to realise that by focusing on the details that feel frustrating (which can't be actioned until the next day), you may be decreasing your ultimate success. Remember, dreaming is the biggest builder of success when you commit to New Dreaming it afterwards.

Perhaps there are other anxieties that can be quieted through speaking to someone, and it's best to do so only if they are in a receptive mood and if you can both carry it through without getting upset or agitated. Many of the issues that you have been allowing to run amok inside your head are often sorted out by the time you awake. As John Steinbeck said, "It is common experience that a problem difficult at night is resolved in the morning after the committee of sleep has worked on it." So hand the dilemma over to the committee of sleep, or to God, or to your unconscious mind, and don't stay up trying to babysit it into submission.

If you are going to bed feeling in a bad mood, one fast way of getting yourself feeling good and a great way to prepare your mind for powerful dreaming is to ask yourself the following questions. You can even journal these or take turns coming up with answers with your bed mate.

- In what ways did I make a difference today?

- Who do I really love, and who loves me?

- What am I grateful for?

- What wonderful things would I most like to dream about tonight?

- What did I learn from today?

- What is the first thing I would like to say when I wake up?

These night questions get you into the kind of emotional and physical state that will ensure you sleep soundly and dream the dreams that will boost your success in life.

In those groggy hypnotically powerful moments before you fall asleep, get in the habit of focusing on one image from your future ultimate life, or one empowering phrase, or one wonderful sound or feeling. Breathe even more deeply and know that this will be your companion for the next eight hours. Choose this companion carefully, as it will be your guide as your conscious mind switches off.

EPILOGUE

"Good night, good night! Parting is such sweet sorrow,
That I shall say good night till it be morrow."
— WILLIAM SHAKESPEARE, *Romeo and Juliet*

Now that You are Sleeping your Way to Success . . .
Now that you know you can change your life by
changing how you sleep, what else would you like to
set in motion?

Now that you have more energy, what amazing
things are you going to do?

How will having all this energy and new
consciousness affect your life?

What else can you do right now that will make
tonight an even more wonderful and powerful night?

So much can be made better with just a little thought
and action, as you have no doubt been discovering.
Now that we are reaching the end of this book I would
like you to take note of the review section following.
This is designed for you to revise, revisit and renew
your incredible new ways of letting success appear in
your life in its many forms.

All kinds of amazing things are already happening while you sleep. Your body is repairing the damage from the day, your unconscious mind is feeding you information in a (usually) entertaining way and letting you know what is going on with your mind. Other great things might be happening too. Some people reading this will be growing new life inside them; some will be wrapped around a person they love; some will be experiencing the warmth and safety they have always yearned for; some will be relieved that they are resting from the challenges of the day. All of us are being carried towards an even richer future, as long as we allow our boat to be steered in good directions through the night. Whatever has been happening with your sleep in the past, you are well on your way to creating even better nights, which will instantly improve your days.

Review

Write up the answers to the following questions as a way of reconnecting with everything you have learned and as a way of taking your sleeping to success to an even higher level. These fun exercises might prompt you to revisit some areas of the book that you feel will further boost your progress.

- What emotional patterns have you changed through adopting new beliefs and through New Dreaming? Lonely to loved, closed and angry to open and communicative, feelings of lack to feelings of abundance?

- What has improved in your life because of this?

- What emotional aspects would you like to enhance further with New Dreaming?

- What are you now letting into the storehouse that you weren't previously? Healthy insights from enlightened people, great books, laughter, beautiful natural scenery?

- What do you now refuse to collect in your storehouse? Malicious gossip, superficial information, violence from the news, distressing sounds, dirt and mess?

- What other positive things would you like in the storehouse to strengthen and guide your journey, and what steps are you taking to ensure that happens?

- Revisit the goals you set, notice your progress, and ask what you might need to do differently, and what you might need to do more or less of in order to achieve those goals:
  - Love relationship
  - Family
  - Friends
  - Career
  - Health and Fitness

o Creativity and Spirituality

o Learning

o Travel

o Money

o Contribution and service.

- What has been your favourite New Dream to date?

- Why?

- What ways have you found to extend and share your New Dreaming? Journaling, treasure-mapping, forming a New Dreaming group?

- What are your new beliefs about yourself as a successful sleeper?

- What do you now do or no longer do that helps you to sleep successfully?

- What hours do you now regularly sleep?

- What gets you up in the morning?

- What further fun and magical things can you weave into your morning routine?

- What changes have you made to your sleep space in terms of sights, sounds, smells, comfort and safety?

- How do these changes make you feel?

- What would you like to do next?

- How do you now dress for bed?

- What old habits have you let go of?

- What better habits have you put in place?

- How do you now help your body in its night-time repairs by what you eat?

- What do you no longer eat and drink?

- What do you now eat and drink more of?

- How do you see yourself further stepping-up over the next week?

- Please tick this box when it is true for you:

  ☐ I am now caffeine free and loving it and excited about all the extra energy I now have for creating my ultimate life.

- How much fun do you now have moving your body so that you will sleep well at night?

- What fun ways to move have you (re)introduced to your life?

- How much water do you drink every day?

- How can you make sure that it remains easy for you to drink water?

- What creative and relaxing things are you finding to do if you are ever awake-at-night?

- In what ways have you become an absolute joy to share a bed or a bedroom with?

- How do you ensure that you and your partner keep the bed as a positive and protected place?

- What routines and guidelines have you set in place regarding your kids' sleep patterns and habits?

- What is your new bedtime routine?

- How does it serve you and your loved ones?

- How much more peaceful is your mind when you get into bed?

- How can you take this to an even more advanced level of pleasure?

I would like to put this book to bed with my wish that you will continue to demand a better quality of life for yourself, that you will dream bigger and better and make your New Dreams come true. As you carry on with your amazing journey I know that you are being an inspiration and a source of comfort and pride to those around you and to the larger world. May you continue to have fun and grow as you sleep your way to success.

Resources

Other self-help resources:
www.SleepingYourWayToSuccess.com
www.OneYearDream.com
www.JudyMayMurphy.TV

Inspirational Movies
The Pursuit of Happyness
Mr Holland's Opus
Dead Poets Society
The Secret
The Bucket List
The Empire Strikes Back
The Edge
Braveheart
Norma Rae
Rocky
How To Make An American Quilt
The Color Purple
Jonathan Livingston Seagull

The following wonderful books are available for free or very cheaply online:
Think and Grow Rich by Napoleon Hill.
The Richest Man in Babylon by George S Clason.
The Science Of Getting Rich by Wallace Wattles.

Here is some further suggested reading:
Believe It and You'll See It by Dr Wayne Dyer.
The Feel Good Handbook by Dr David Burnes (very long and comprehensive).
Co-Dependent No More by Melody Beattie.
Your Erroneous Zones by Wayne Dyer.
Learned Optimism by Martin Seligman (more academic style).
Caffeine Blues by Stephen Cherniske.
Conquering Caffeine Dependence by Mike Fillon.